The Fascist Nature of Neoliberalism

Capitalism is based on a false logic in which all facts and ideas are reduced to a consideration of their 'feasibility' within the capitalist system. Thus, all mainstream economic and political theories, including those such as Marxism which are supposed to offer an alternative vision, have been stunted and utopian ideas are completely side-lined. In order to constantly work out the feasible, you have to hang on to pseudo-factual concepts: nationalism; a constant drive for efficiency; the idea of nation/state; corporatism; managed markets; business ethics; governance; and so on. Capitalism is reduced to the management of the economy by states that fight each other and marvel at the independence of finance. All this, the book argues, is akin, intellectually, economically, politically and, unfortunately, individually to fascism.

The Fascist Nature of Neoliberalism offers a brief, provocative analysis of this issue with special reference to the most visible executioners of its will: the much-misunderstood managerial class. This group simply happens to hold power, and hence visibility, but they do what everybody else does, and would do, all the time. This is because capitalism is an intellectual outlook that thoroughly directs individual actions through fascist and non-fascist repression. This book argues that the only way to escape capitalism is to recover individual intellectual and sentimental emancipation from capitalism itself in order to produce radical solutions.

This volume is of great importance to those who study and are interested in political economy, economic theory and philosophy, as well as fascism and neoliberalism.

Andrea Micocci is Professore Straordinario di Economia Politica at Link University, Rome, Italy.

Flavia Di Mario taught at Link Campus University and Sole24 Business School and was Guest Speaker at Loyola University and American University of Rome. She is now pursuing her PhD studying Political Economy, Industrial Relations.

Routledge Frontiers of Political Economy

The Fascist Nature of Neoliberalism

Andrea Micocci and Flavia Di Mario

Routledge
Taylor & Francis Group

LONDON AND NEW YORK

First published 2018
by Routledge

2 Park Square, Milton Park, Abingdon, Oxfordshire OX14 4RN

52 Vanderbilt Avenue, New York, NY 10017

Routledge is an imprint of the Taylor & Francis Group, an informa business

First issued in paperback 2020

British Library Cataloguing-in-Publication Data
A catalogue record for this book is available from the British Library

Library of Congress Cataloging-in-Publication Data
Names: Micocci, Andrea, author. | Di Mario, Flavia, author.
Title: The fascist nature of neoliberalism / Andrea Micocci and
Flavia Di Mario.
Description: 1 Edition. | New York: Routledge, 2018. |
Includes bibliographical references and index.
Identifiers: LCCN 2017037156 | ISBN 9780815369882 (hardback) |
ISBN 9781351251204 (ebook)
Subjects: LCSH: Capitalism. | Economic policy. | Neoliberalism. |
Fascism.
Classification: LCC HB501 .M6265 2018 | DDC 330.12/2—dc23
LC record available at https://lccn.loc.gov/2017037156

ISBN: 978-0-8153-6988-2 (hbk)
ISBN: 978-0-367-59428-2 (pbk)

Typeset in Times New Roman
by Cenveo Publisher Services

Contents

Acknowledgements

We have received, as usual, a lot of help for what we were planning to write, for the work we submit to the public here has been in the making for many years and has not seen its final form until certain themes were settled and certain evident absurdities had become impossible to bear. In the first place, we thankfully acknowledge numerous hostile commentators, who aided us in improving our text by considering their points of view. Second, we gratefully thank Alessandro Micocci, David Micocci, Nino Pardjanadze, Edmundo de Werna Magalhaes, Mino Vianello, Brunella Antomarini, Nadine Valat and Claudio Micocci. Charles McCann needs very special thanks from us. Third, we thank everybody at Routledge, especially Andy Humphries. None of the above are, of course, responsible for anything we hereby say. Flavia Di Mario would like to acknowledge some material originating in her PhD dissertation under way at Middlesex University, and the people involved in it, with the same proviso as above. Also, she would like to thank her family in Rome, Tiziana and Ileana Nardoni, Andrea Palomba and Federica Simoncioni and the Cosentino and Camille families. A very special thanks to Kelvin Asare-Williams and the Junior Art Club members and communities in Ghana that hosted her. This work she dedicates to the loving memory of a fervent anti-fascist, her grandmother Rosa Di Lernia. Andrea Micocci would also like to thank, without any responsibility on their part, all his students at all institutions and countries where he taught: without them, he would have written nothing. If we have forgotten anybody, we beg forgiveness.

Foreword

The present work has been written in order to dispel some likely illusions present-day debates are bound to induce, changing the truthful features of reality. To be fair in our judgement, we have made an effort, therefore, to go to the core of the questions at stake, and we have found it to be an unpleasant core. As a consequence, what we are going to say might be taxing to those who are used to, or who are happy with, the present state of things. We are going to argue that capitalism, in its latest, neoliberal, version, is not what liberal and communist thinkers alike thought it would become. Instead, it has some telling characteristics that make it similar, in fact, to what fascist and Catholic/Christian political movements have dreamt. In what follows, we have left aside the Christian movements because, unlike the fascists, their action is claimed to be ruled by a rigid set of moral laws with a universal value, criticism of which evidently requires a completely different type of argument.

The above and much more was not lost on J.A. Schumpeter (see especially his 1987, 2013), who sought to argue throughout his life that capitalism could become a proper market, with all the economic and political benefits entailed, only if what he called 'development' were entrusted to creativity and revolution, what is vulgarly known as the process of 'creative destruction'. While restating this creative starting point in his *Capitalism, Socialism and Democracy* (1942 [1987]), only to admit that, to his experience, it never came true, he clearly sees that there is a 'hostility to the capitalist order' (p. 143). The bourgeoisie is 'a whole scheme of bourgeois values', which matters only in theory. The actual bourgeois class in fact is 'ill-equipped' (p. 138) to face problems of any importance. Protection by 'some non-bourgeois group is needed'. This point is basic in what follows. Schumpeter made the big mistake, however, of concluding that the managerial class would die with the growth of capitalist rationality. We shall show in the pages that follow that, with neoliberalism, it has, instead, transmogrified into a new fascist militia, often willingly mistaken as being coextensive with the entrepreneurial classes. What follows is all about finding the meaning of these prophecies, wrong and right.

The theoretical premise at the origin of what we argue here is based on the work of a couple of decades by Andrea Micocci. In it, as explained in Micocci (2002, 2009/2010, 2012, 2016), capitalism is based on an intellectuality (we call it here a metaphysics, following Micocci, 2009/2010, 2016) that is logically flawed and limited. The (flawed) logic of exchanges, for instance, supersedes and even replaces actual exchanges. That is, exchanges can or cannot happen, while their intellectual presence drives the whole of human behaviour, much as the intellectuality of love and sex are supposed to guide sentimental relationships but are rarely mentioned by lay people. In other words, actual facts are helped, or even replaced, by their capitalistic permissibility. Without it, capitalist intercourses would be too complex, which is a point to which many mainstream scholars would be willing to subscribe. It also is, more importantly for us here, incapable of producing radical arguments – that is, non-capitalist arguments. As a consequence, the radical, revolutionary power of the capitalist transformation itself, based upon utopian visions (take, for the most absurd, the perfect market), has been stunted. The same has happened to alternative visions of human society – for instance, Marxism. They all have lost their capacity to produce radical arguments – that is, of making revolutions.

The result is that all the mainstream theories and, most importantly, the practices related to economics and politics had to resort to the perfectly absurd *a priori* chimera of 'the feasible', or the realistic, or whatever you might want to call such an empty idea. In fact, one can judge what is feasible and realistic only after it has, or has not, been done. Yet, all political and economic theories strive to only propose, do and dream of the feasible. They are never hit by the simple fact that such a claim is even more utopian and unjustified than the perfect market, anarchism or communism. Fascists and neoliberals, we shall see, are masters at that.

In order constantly to work out the feasible, you have to hang on to pseudo-factual concepts. To do so, history must be, and has been, disfigured to dig up supposedly constant features in human history which, however, appear constant and human only when looked at from the capitalist perspective. Marx himself taught us the relevance of this basic historical hypostatisation. Such mistakes respond to the capitalist metaphysics, however, and are functional to it: they count only in capitalism, to the extent you buy, and use, its flawed and limiting logic. Nationalism and its constituent parts (efficiency, as the lubricated functioning of things social, organic society, the idea of nation/state, corporatism, a managed market, the confusion between capitalism and free economic initiative helped by the state, a social ethic, a business ethic, governance and the like) are at the core of this vision that is repeated *ad nauseam* and with all possible variations by everybody, including people who call themselves liberal or communist.

Capitalism is reduced to the management of the economy by states that fight each other and marvel at the independence of finance, which instead is the most obvious consequence of the flawed logic of profit, as we shall see. (For a thorough historical and philosophical demonstration, however, see Micocci, 2011a, 2011b, 2016.) All this, we argue in what follows, is akin, intellectually, economically, politically and, unfortunately, individually (for it involves, to be believed, sexual repression sustained in time) to fascism. Indeed, the best interpreter and manager of the spirit of 'capitalism as we know it' today is fascism in all its different brands. In what follows, we offer a brief, first approach to this question with reference to the present neoliberal capitalism and to the most visible executioners of its will, the much misunderstood managerial class. These last epitomise, in the mean poverty of their mentality and practical action, what everybody else does in our times. We are very keen on this last aspect: the managerial class simply happens to hold power and hence visibility, but they do what everybody else does, and would do, all the time. This is because capitalism is a metaphysics, an intellectual outlook that thoroughly directs individual actions (Micocci, 2016). In it, the poor are, theoretically, potentially and actually, as bad as the rich. Only, they hold no power.

Our message here is that the only way out of capitalism is to recover individual intellectual and sentimental emancipation from capitalism itself. Only then will we be able to produce radical solutions that do not require fascist and non-fascist repression. A warning is therefore needed to those who feel ready to read the pages that follow: acknowledging the fascist nature of capitalism is only the first step. We hope, with this short work, to start a reaction rather than one more useless debate.

1 Introduction

The financial problem is the crucial problem: we must balance
the state budget as soon as possible.

Benito Mussolini, first speech as Prime Minister[1]

Few economists and lay persons are bound to disagree when
someone says that capitalism cannot be a functioning market
economy unless it is supported by a state, a juridical system and
a conflict-solving social and political organisation – and 'market',
here, can be meant in the common, approximate and vague way
we all use in our daily business, as well as in the sense stated in
microeconomic theory. Nor would anybody disagree if the
necessity of a degree of homogeneity and efficiency – a sense of
common purpose – is judged necessary. To this, one can also
safely add that an unspecified quantity of conflicts and disagree-
ments are bound to remain, which must be, and usually are,
tamed into the feasible. Most lay people would say that the
above is simply the essence of reality. Very significantly, they are
unlikely to say 'this is what reality looks like', for that would
imply doubt of the truthfulness, and response to human needs, of
everything that has been said.

Competent and politically aware economists, as a consequence, would find attempts to go beyond this apparently innoc-
uous generalisation in the direction of exploring the general
features of actual capitalist states, juridical systems and social
and political organisations hard to digest. They are scared by the
intuition that capitalism is not quite the same thing implicit in

economic and political theories, which is what we are going to argue in the pages that follow. Capitalism, neoliberalism and fascism are, to the chagrin of these self-secure economists, fuzzy and even self-contradictory. We are going to show this protean aspect, for it is there that explanations must be found – difficult explanations.

We propose in what follows that 'capitalism as we know it' today is akin to, and indeed partakes in the same nature as, fascist ideas and actual practices about politics and the economy.[2] Both fascism and capitalism as we know it, in fact, imply an organic society (a community, as present-day capitalist men and women of all political persuasions are fond to say[3]); trade unions that are fought and repressed until they are tamed into a corporatist structure and strategy; a role for a social/socialised ethics and even a business ethics that is sought and even (in some historical periods) surprisingly found; war as a means to resolve thorny international relations issues; horror towards forms of sociality that are not based on the standard capitalist state; the perception of the 'other' as either a threat or an ally; and a tension between politics and the economy, easy to brand as an efficiency problem. This guilty confusion takes place, as we will argue repeatedly, because otherness is disregarded in that it is replaced with diversity, as in Hegel (2008). (See Micocci 2016.) All the above cannot be understood without this fundamental trait being always in our minds. In capitalism, all problems can be mediated because there is no 'other' reality, but only 'capitalist' diversity. We will see this, with further important particulars, in Chapter 2 and onwards.

In order for the majority to leave well enough alone and go on with pointless but feasible debates, language and logic are distorted and, above all, limited: they are transformed into what Cassirer (1962) called 'mythical language'. In more general terms (Micocci, 2016), metaphysics[4] and myth replace sound ideas: vague capitalistic concepts replace concrete facts, as well as abstract reasoning in the (paradoxical) name of efficiency coupled with flexibility. Evocation rather than definition is, in other words, practised.[5] This, to us – and to many other authors – is fascism, as we shall see in Chapter 3.

In other words, a flawed, limited and limiting (fascist) metaphysics informs present-day capitalism of itself. Economic theory, due to its logically flawed structure that mirrors such dominant intellectuality, is condemned to be part of such metaphysics, never to transcend it in any way.[6] Marxist theories could have gained intellectual independence from all that, had the banally metaphysical – and wrong – Hegelian mentality of those who presided over the Marxist debate not gained overwhelming dominance (Micocci, 2002, 2009/10, 2012, 2016). Their activity has thus helped enhance the fascist character of the metaphysics of capitalism and helped capitalism survive.

As a consequence of all the above, to operate successfully in capitalism you are better off if you hold, and use, a simplified framework for analysis. This latter implies, however, a tremendous complication in the definition of the technicalities because these, as a consequence of the simplifications, are always underdetermined (see Micocci, 2016). Mainstream economics and mainstream Marxism(s) have for long supplied such framework, but they have now been superseded, we argue here, by the much more coherent neoliberal lack of ideas. Neoliberalism is not even a consistent corpus of ideas; in fact, it exists only as a tireless producer of eclectic economic policies. As an outcome, we will see, in due course, it is the best interpreter of the fascist component of the capitalist metaphysics. The alleged liberal features of neoliberal capitalism (for instance, inequality, individual competition, the rolling back of the welfare state and of the planning activity of the state in the economy, firm management), as we will show, perfectly fit the fascist nature of capitalism theoretically as well as historically, and depend on the presence of its mythical language. (Take 'the regulating power of the market' locution for a typical instance.)

The recent preponderance of finance (Micocci, 2011a, 2011b, 2012, 2016) has powerfully helped this trend by enhancing the grip of the dominant metaphysics of profits on actual capitalist life and on its mythical language (Di Mario and Micocci, 2015). Firm management and, as a consequence of neoliberal stupidity, even state management are imbibed with such mentality.[7] The two things have grown hand in hand. The enhancement of the metaphysics produced by the financialisation induced by neoliberalism has spread itself even on the wretched classes, which do not partake of the financial bonanza. Authoritarian forms of democracy and populist solutions can thus be imposed on whole populations, as Europe has shown so well as to need no further explanation. Proportional electoral representation has virtually disappeared from the world.[8]

This text, against much of the present fashion, is not going to argue that the present crisis that started in 2007 has brought anything relevantly new to the scenario we are going to depict. This is because crises are normal to the development of capitalism and come down to capitalist conflicts, which are unable to produce any novelty, despite the rhetoric of all the prophets of doom who proliferate in such circumstances. The features of capitalism that matter to us remain the same despite all the human sufferings such crises entail. Also, as we will show in Chapter 3, fascist economic and political programmes are so shallow, vague and eclectic as to emasculate any economic and political challenge, however violent or damaging. Fascism is violent because its politics is impotent.

In Chapter 2, we outline the theory behind this book, thus describing the relevant features of capitalism as we know it.

In Chapter 3, we discuss fascism, basing our argument mainly but not solely on Italian fascism. We shall seek to emphasise the relevant economic and political features of fascism in general in order to see its relation with capitalism.

Chapter 4 discusses neoliberalism in the light of what has been said in the preceding pages. It shows how capitalism, fascism and neoliberalism are perfectly parallel and share in the same nature.

Chapter 5 presents a peculiar feature of neoliberalism, which helps it survive by enhancing some of its fascistic features: managerialism.

The conclusions will be as brief as possible because the fascist features of capitalism as we know it and of its present-day version called neoliberalism have been, hopefully, demonstrated in the course of the argument.

An edifying little story is told in the Appendix to help the reader in trouble understand the guilty subtlety and vulgarity of the whole through the example of academia, which should nurture, besides intellectual erudition, originality, but instead contributes, we hold, to the present state of things. With such belief we offer it.

Notes

1 In Mussolini (1934).
2 Many will seek to criticise us by claiming that our use of the word fascism is too personal and idiosyncratic. By it, however, we mean what we say here, and we know no other term for it. Polemics about it are therefore specious, or political. For a fruitful discussion of populism, an inadequate but fashionable item that helps further distortions, see D'Eramo (2013).
3 For a critique of the indiscriminate use of the concept of community, see Micocci (2012).
4 '[A]n intellectual construction that aims to provide an ultimate system of meaning to reality' (Micocci, 2016, p. 1). Things are reduced to capitalist things, whence their limited and limiting role, and nature itself, is perfectly out of touch.
5 For the theoretical background to this general reasoning, see Micocci (2016).
6 Its theoretical features are a logically analogous metaphysics to the capitalist metaphysics (see Micocci, 2002, 2009/10, 2012, 2016).
7 By the way, to the chagrin of Sweezy (1962), Burnham (1942) was well aware of this feature.
8 A pure proportional system probably existed only in Italy, and was abolished at the dawn of the neoliberal era with the criminal impulse and action of the Communist Party (PCI). See Abse (1993).

2 Capitalism

Capitalism has been conceptualised in two main ways by those who have studied its economy: as a concentration of commodities based upon a labour-exploiting M-C-M' (money-commodity-money') (with M'>M) dynamic by Marxists, or as a set of continuous, fair commercial exchanges intrinsic to human nature (hence the need to devise and produce endless quantities of commodities of all qualities) by the neoclassicals, and more recntly by their successors, the so-called 'mainstream economists'. We utilise here, as already said, an alternative to both, developed in Micocci (2002, 2009/10, 2012, 2016): capitalism as metaphysics, which we briefly reiterate in what follows. By doing this, we will outline the most relevant features of capitalism as we know it.

Capitalism as we know it, as everybody knows, has come to acquire its present characteristics because its evolution over time, as the mainstream and mainstream Marxist(s) accounts as well propose, produced a historical rift in the Middle Ages with an entailed, correspondent change in the mode of production. The coherence and resilience of such change, however (and here we part from all mainstream accounts), as it is human beings who perform economic and political activities, can only be explained by observing the homogenisation of the intellectual *modus operandi* of each individual agent as well as private and public institutions that has taken place over the said historical period. States and markets have further helped the spread of such intellectual homogenisation of the individual by acquiring 'capitalistic' features. Indeed, if there existed, however limited in size and importance, any pockets of alternative intellectual structures endowed with the entailed alternative ways to articulate thought, imagine things and see and feel them, capitalism as we know it would have been challenged to its core. This last is constituted by the presumed correspondence, mainly spread for our purposes here by the mainstream, of capitalism as we know it with the needs and wants of human nature, and its capacity to rule them efficiently, for the good and the bad.

As a consequence, present-day capitalism consists in an *a priori*, general intellectual framework that allows individuals and institutions to make sense, relate and narrate natural and political facts alike. Nature and the social world share an unspecified common nature, thus excusing capitalism. Simultaneously, this big intellectual mistake also supplies a general logic and methodology for understanding and pigeon-holing anything that might come forth as yet 'unknown'. This is what we call a metaphysics. Such metaphysics replaces all former similar and analogous structures of thought, or the system (capitalism as we know it as a human, hence natural, outcome) would not work as a whole. In other words, it substitutes the former potential, as well as actual diversity of thought structures with its general, pervasive and 'scientific' methodology. Such metaphysics, we argue, with Marx in general, Colletti (1975), Della Volpe (1969), Rosenthal (1998), Micocci (2002, 2009/2010, 2016), is of the vulgar Hegelian kind.

Without its homogenising power, the endless economic and political exchanges based on commodity production that the neoclassical and Marxists have individuated would not take place. Non-capitalist countries and individuals must bend to it: they want to pretend to act in favour of or against capitalism, but anything they do or say must and only can be practised along the lines of the dominant mentality, or cannot be communicated. This is what Marx and Engels (1975) pointed out in many places, starting with the metaphorical metonymy of the 'heavy artillery' of the bourgeoisie destroying all Chinese Walls in the Manifesto of the Communist Party (ibid., p. 39) and finishing with their often repeated triple alienation (from oneself, other men and nature).

If this logical homogeneity spread all over the world is the basic requirement and qualifying feature for the existence of capitalism, it is very important to notice, before we describe it in any more detail, that – whatever capitalism's virtues and flaws – it must necessarily determine, at the individual as well as at the social level, a distorting selection and reduction of emotional reactions. Not only are individuals limited and distorted in their sensual perceptions and in their capacity to devise new, revolutionary[1] conceptions, but also the capitalist complete homogeneity at the global and, more likely and relevantly for what we are bound to say, at the national level cause a socialised chain reaction. All this can also go on because, despite the banality of wireless communication in present-day capitalism, the nation-state is still the main reference for individuals. Similarity generates similarity, repression generates repression, in a typical intellectual and psychological sequence à la Wilhelm Reich (1970).

The main characteristics produced by the dominant metaphysics of capitalism have been well individuated, once again, by both the mainstream economists and by Marx.[2] They are simply and evidently, and briefly, what economic theories of all brands talk about. To discuss the ones we need here, we shall use Marx's own language because its wider methodological nature involves psychology and philosophy in addition to history. This course of action, it is well worth pointing out, takes us far away from the Marxist mainstream(s) instead of getting us closer to it. (See Chapter 1, note 8 again.)

The most important aspect of capitalist functioning – that is, of the capitalist metaphysics – is that, as pointed out by many (Feuerbach and Marx in the first place), it is a poor, vulgarly Hegelian thing. The consequences of this characterising feature are tremendously important, in general, and especially to explain the fascist nature of whatever we end up calling 'capitalism as we know it' (Micocci, 2002, 2009/10, 2012, 2016). Capitalist logic is, as a consequence, perfectly incapable of conceiving ruptures and disappearances: that is to say, by way of an example, Kantian real oppositions (Micocci, 2002; Della Volpe, 1969; Colletti, 1975). The whole universe is conceived of as a place where only mediations take place. As in Hegel's *Phenomenology of Spirit* (2008), various degrees of difference replace the fact of otherness, substituting continuously. Nonetheless, deviously, the very word 'otherness' is purposely kept and even continuously (mis)used, in place of the more correct diversity and/or mediation. The consequences of this logical mistake are at the basis of capitalism itself and of its violence and prevarication, as well as of its impossibility to devise revolutionary (i.e. radical) alternatives from inside itself (see Micocci, 2002, 2012, 2016).

Not only are politics and economics based on a continuous reciprocal mediation between those sole items that are allowed, and hence perceived, to constitute reality, as hinted earlier. The natural sciences, and material reality, also follow the same general logic: they tend towards a high point of arrival that excludes certain inadequate items, and they pursue their set path by dialectically interacting. Conflict and mediation having been collapsed together, each (supposed) object of reality is a (Hegelian) mixture of the determinations that have contributed to its contrivance, even when only the winning determination(s) are visible. It is precisely this great moderation, the metaphysical homogeneity of the forces at work both in nature and in society, that allows all sciences to use the same method, and therefore contribute towards the achievement of that high goal (say, perfect capitalism or any alternative to it or, say, sustainability). Conflicts appear as constitutive of reality, and impossible to quell. Yet, they are never solutions, let alone revolutionary, in their action.

Little wonder, then, that the narrative accounts of capitalism as we know it – be them scientific as mainstream economics or Marxist and heterodox political economy or political as ideologies (in our case, fascism) – bear little relationship to material reality.[3] Rather than the material objects of which the world is supposed made, all narrative accounts must, as with all actual economic intercourses, represent, convey and use the corresponding intellectual (metaphysical) concept. Such concept can only be dialectical and mediate with other concepts rather than with material reality. To use Marx's jargon, objects 'conceived in thought' interact, justified by the general belief that this is a common perception – that is, that material reality evolves by the same dialectical mechanisms. The consequences are momentous and ominous, and act upon actual reality: actually living and suffering material objects and creatures.

Such material objects and creatures have been stripped, as said, of their material status and have been intellectually endowed with a new, metaphysical nature that characterises them as the bearers of certain properties, some of which can be traced back to their material origin (e.g. the production process or the raw materials required to obtain commodities, their nutritional value, their resistance to use), while others are fully metaphysical in theory and in fact (e.g. the unfounded notion that the internet is about information, the ethical value of your purchase, its responding to fashion's dictates, business ethics, individual opinion, private property). In this second group, it is fundamental to stress, there can be found items that are intellectually perceived to be as basic to managing life as those of a material origin: take the 'necessity' to have political stability, a balanced state budget, a mobile phone or a car or a bicycle if you are ecologically so inclined. (We have chosen here, for the purpose of the present work, representative present-day declinations of efficiency.) We can summarise this double set of characteristics as the general feature of everything to be amenable to a commodity-like[4] kind of treatment, again using Marx's own words throughout his life. This is also Marx's triple alienation from yourself, your fellow humans and nature, generalised to the whole universe.

Thus, the reason capitalism can be likened to a huge heap of commodities – which Marx, just as (indirectly) the neoclassical, appeared to propose[5] – is not because of the actual existence of any such heap, and most certainly not because of the actual existence of its qualifying material features. What matters is that we think, and act, as if anything, comprising our feelings, were treatable by the same logic, which happens to be the same in that it is the only one, and it is logically and naturally identical to that of commodity production and exchange. This does not mean, it is very important to point out, that all objects and feelings are commodities: the very contrary is true. Objects and feelings, which have been, in the first place, as noticed earlier, limited, reduced and selected in number and quality by the metaphysics of capitalism, or the whole thing would be too complex and risky, are thought about, traded and used, in theory just as in everyday life, by using the same intellectual mechanistic methods that are used for commodities. The very same intellectual logic, correctly identified by Marx and even by the Marxists as dialectical, is used all the time, in the strenuous attempt to keep off the simple and evident fact of nature that ruptures with disappearances do exist, and that they may happen at any time, uncovering the guilty folly of capitalist metaphysics.[6]

The language that is spoken in capitalist economic intercourse, and in its institutions, juridical systems and political and social customs, is as a consequence perfectly and completely metaphysical.[7] The material origin and use of things is forgone, and is replaced by the metaphysics itself with its homogenising power. This last allows the description of complexity because it calls complex what is not complex but simply logically flawed. Science contributes by devising theories that are always dialectical and ape the dialectics of actual capitalism and of its analysis by the social sciences and the other way around. To name a fashionable instance, equilibrium, a fundamental concept in ecology, erases the possibility of evolution by erasing ruptures with disappearances (Micocci, 2016). As a consequence, everybody feels safe, for nature can be tamed and even rescued. Or, diseases – rather than cured, avoided or erased – are dialectically interacted with by administering medicines, whether they are effective or not.

Human interactions, we repeat, are completely entrusted to the dominant metaphysics, which, despite the apparent abundance of degrees of difference in actual facts, discourses and analyses, argues homogeneously. Thus, institutions, juridical systems and those collective behaviours that capitalism is capable of recording are hypostatised as the only way for human collective action to exist. Organic societies, to take a typical fascist[8] dream (but we could just as easily take the market, or private property), come to life as incontrovertible concepts – that is, capitalist apparent objects and matters of fact. The natural consequence of all this is that no revolution is possible. Only similar systems can replace those systems that are being scrapped by popular revolt or by external intervention. In a perfectly vulgar Hegelian fashion, subversion (diversity in all its degrees) is mistaken for revolution (otherness). The pressing need to preserve these non-different differences explains the need to use violence both if you are in favour and if you are against any such happening (Micocci, 2012). Thus violence cannot be a self-sustaining factor in describing any ideology of capitalist times. Fundamentally for us here, reactionary as well as progressive revolts have, therefore, the same claim to be named revolutions or ideologies: there is no alternative otherness at work, even when everybody knows they are not 'other' and put up with it for social or personal reasons.

One of the most representative features of the metaphysics of capitalism is, as accepted by all economic theories, the use and understanding of prices and values, and the need for money. Money becomes the most perfect dialectical mediation means to ensure the institutionalisation, interchangeability, repeatability and (useless) communicability of everything under capitalism. Prices and values refer equally well to shoes, potatoes, social, natural and human capital, loss of limbs or of lives (one of the authors has lost a leg and is being compensated for the relative loss of working capacity), wages, ideas and what have you. The presumed mystery of the transformation of values into prices is resolved in practice all the time by citizens, while economists agonise over the mathematical conundrums of its theoretical description (Micocci, 2008). Yet, if money performs this vital role of producing, expressing and embodying value, mark-up and rent, why should material production, still anchored to its ancestral material origin, not be superseded by the straight M-M' circuit we find in Marx?[9]

Finance, in fact, grants rates of profit that are not tied to the unavoidable physical, chemical and human limits of material production. Capital is the most perfectly metaphysical concept we find in the capitalist metaphysics, in theory and in practice. It is an intellectual concept with an independent life of its own, which any of us can hold, gain or lose. Hence, its preponderance today, with the entailed de-industrialisation of the developed countries and the transferral of material production to the Third World, which holds, or pursues, an obsolete type of capitalism.

Finance can only be understood, and properly utilised, when it is conceived, as professional analysts and tycoons (and, surprisingly, common people) do, exclusively within the borders of the metaphysics. Only then does it correspond to something usable in 'capitalist reality'. Its logic and language are so coherent with the general logic of capitalism that they become preponderant and easy to understand for competent and incompetent people alike.[10] The rough logic of managerial power can thus display, as we will see, all its practical power. There also are endless fields for its application.[11] Take the most insulting: the Stalinist ideas of social, human or natural capital, which everybody uses without qualms today.

The above is a serious challenge for mainstream economics and mainstream Marxism(s). After having conquered for themselves a fully metaphysical structure[12] since the end of the nineteenth century, they have suddenly found themselves tied to the direct (for political economy) and indirect (for the economic mainstream, which has the detour of basing itself on exchanges, which, in turn, presuppose commodities) material (natural and human) origin of commodities. They thus miss the simplicity of the M-M' (M'>M) circuit, which is the true, evident solution to the material complications M-C-M' offers to those who are after a profit – that is, everybody, comprising the waged worker, the unemployed and the delinquent.[13]

Managerial capitalism[14] thus faces a double challenge: the convenience of quitting material productions, and even commerce and services, to enter finance. As a consequence, we witness the need to tighten up production conditions and processes to face the change in the flows of capital, keeping profit as high as possible in order to slow down the lure of finance for material producers.

Production is outsourced and transferred where pillage and slavery are possible; the Third World is plundered for raw materials more than ever before (even for new products due to new fashions, such as the guilty vegan craze. Take just the sad, international quinoa instance, as discussed by Berson, 2014); and the working class is attacked, over-exploited and deprived of trade union rights. States and juridical systems go along with this game in the desperate attempt to save their GDP growth rates and to keep the other macroeconomic fundamentals at non-socially dangerous levels. Ideologies endorse all this, just as they endorsed the welfare state earlier. The World Bank (WB) and the IMF indulge in, and even invent, the language everybody copies at the international level (Moretti and Pestre, 2015). People understand both horns of the dilemma, which they transform into a lottery type of life (Di Mario and Micocci, 2015). The growing threat of social unrest enhances the intrinsic corporatism of capitalist institutions (take the state, trade unions, industrial associations and the authoritarian downturn of the Western democracies). Again, intellectuals and economic theories endorse all this, as they did for the preceding alternatives. Social peace and ethics in banking and business appear, as a consequence, as reasonable and possible solutions instead of what they are: fascist ideas.

Also, open corporatist tendencies that had been kept at bay by the post-war boom resurface. Indeed, they never disappeared because they have granted an unspoken support to the untenability of the mainstream and mainstream Marxist(s) notions and understanding of the firm, the market and industrial relations. Schumpeter's speech of 1945 in Montreal in (1993) that scandalised Samuelson (ibid.) best exemplifies this corporatist attitude, which has also been transferred, in part and with the due modifications, to Galbraith's 'technostructure' and to what we shall refer to later as managerial capitalism. Certainly, in the present day of financialised capitalism, the state operates in close touch with industry, the tertiary sector and even agriculture (Micocci, 2016; Di Mario, 2015); indeed, they chime in unison (Galbraith, 2009; Gallino, 2011; Micocci, 2016). Corporatism is back in the open, and it is here to stay because even governments and parties that pretend not to be capitalist (say, the various Latin American instances collectively named '*socialismo indigena*', or the Tsipras fake in Greece, Podemos in Spain, M5S and the PD in Italy) look for a collaboration among what Mussolini called the corporations, and social peace. All they want is the growth of GDP and the entailed good-looking numbers for the macroeconomic fundamentals: the realistic and feasible.

We can now summarise this complex reasoning, showing those concepts that are compatible with both fascism and neoliberalism. Capitalism is based upon a metaphysics – that is, a socially justified, tranquillising flawed intellectuality that is grounded, to survive, on the pretence that it corresponds to some natural tendencies and instincts of human beings. Reason is, in other words, insufficient unless it is backed by instinct in the fascist sense. As a consequence, all this perfect razzmatazz is socialised rather than individualist. The metaphysics identifies it all in a fascist way.

Second, there is not much of a need for coherence; on the contrary, approximation helps in practice. Action is what counts, it seems, as all mainstream economists and mainstream Marxists would say. Action and efficiency are one and the same thing. This has been captured most precisely by the fascists (and many more, unfortunately) with their idea of 'action' and, worse, 'pure action'. Capitalism as we know it needs an organic sense of society, and this is predicated upon the only 'practical' way to pursue it: the nation. All sorts of bland and hard nationalisms result in being acceptable, just as do unspoken nationalisms – the 'they and us' we know well for the issues of immigration and terrorism, for instance. The state oversees this 'organic community' and the popular will, with *ad hoc* referenda. (One should call them more precisely, with D'Eramo, 2013, plebiscites.)

It follows that both traditionalism and anti-traditionalisms are allowed, for revolution is declared to be banal subversion. Mass consensus is also inevitable, or at least exercised through a single party in power, granting stability as in all majoritarian electoral systems. Individuals can be different, for otherness is inconceivable and, precisely from this diversity, with its dialectical interaction, political debates stem: but action rules, and power must act unhindered (this type of efficiency is often called political stability or governance).[15] Inequality (but remember, diversity, not otherness), even of the economic type, is therefore conducive to the full exercise of economic and political intercourses.

If things are as above, then the state must embody, at least to a degree (capitalism lives and thrives out of things pursued 'to a degree', whatever that might mean in logical thinking), a 'common will', a generalised ethics that prevents moralistic criticisms of injustice. A leader or a leading party in power is a useful, although not indispensable, tool: he/she/it needs not be a dictator, but just an efficient interpreter of the common will (the limited and limiting metaphysics) abiding the common ethics. The 'others' are not part of the organic group, by their decision or by popular will. The masses are, in other words, homogeneous in feelings, ideas and will, and ready to react to anything, for their lust for material (but do not forget that in capitalism material means metaphysical) commodities cannot be moderated. These are, not by chance, the main conditions for the perfect market to exist in theory: but we have seen that, in capitalism as we know it, the theory–reality dichotomy does not exist, and does not matter. In the metaphysics of capitalism, perfect freedom and perfect deception overlap. This we call fascism.

Notes

1 Anything new is necessarily revolutionary in reality. But this never happens in capitalism as we know it because, in the capitalist metaphysics, the new is invisible and conflicts are dialectical (Micocci, 2016). The word 'radical' can be used as well, instead of 'revolutionary'.

2 The difference between Marx and the Marxists is a fundamental issue here that cannot, unfortunately, be discussed. See Micocci, 2016.

3 This aspect has been exploited for decades by those who criticise mainstream theories, to no result, obviously. See Micocci (2002, 2009/2010, 2012, 2016) for some summaries concerning various disciplines.

4 'Alternative' behaviours, which we easily find in capitalism, fully partake in this commodity-like mentality. Take those who claim, as do many green-minded people, that replacing a technique with another is a non-, or even anti-capitalist thing.

5 In *Capital* (1977), Vol. 1, chapter 1, for a popular instance.

6 This in capitalism: in general, however, there are good grounds to hypothesise the presence of the undetermined as well. But this is another more complex and radical story thoroughly considered in its important consequences in Micocci (2016).

7 Everett (2016) has put forward, among other things, a similar but linguistic argument on the diversity of languages and dark matter which we find important enough to point out. He also criticises the so-called 'scientific' mind with arguments that are not very dissimilar from ours.

8 All through this text we take fascism to be necessarily a historically capitalist object.

9 For instance, in *Capital*, Vol. 3 (1977). See Micocci, 2011a, 2011b, 2016.

10 See, for instance, Dore (2009), Posner (2010), Gallino (2011), Davis (2016).

11 Take Moretti and Pestre (2015) for an illustration applied to the WB, and Micocci (2016) for a general treatment.

12 Which in Marxist theory is perfectly unjustified in its dialectical nature; it cannot be found in Marx's own writings (Micocci, 2016).

13 The above is standard treatment Micocci has been offering for years now in various shapes in his publications and in all due ways. Smithin (2016) recently uses it without acknowledgement for reasons other than Micocci's argument (monetary theory), producing an equation involving Y (GDP, real): M-Y-M'. In his treatment, if M=M', or even M'>M, not only there is no incentive to produce (no Y, in other words), but we would be left with M-M': 'all borrowed money goes to financial speculation ... This is a major worry for economists of all political persuasions' (p. 1265). He offers no acknowledgement to Micocci simply because he is discussing a thing no economist wants to hear, in the right and in the left. Yet it is real, or we would not be offering it, and using it without acknowledgement is an academic malpractice.

14 We can take as an exemplary and indicative instance for the purposes of this chapter J.K. Galbraith's 'technostructure'. See Galbraith, 1972, 1983. More on its contemporary development, features and literature in Chapter 5.

15 Imagine a perfectly democratic country, with two or even three parties with perfectly opposing ideologies that alternate in power. Who would want to invest in such an 'uncertain' political environment, especially from abroad?

3 Fascism

The needs of post-World War II reconstruction have led to entrusting the historical meaning of fascism to the description and discussion of its most tragic outcomes: dictatorship, war, massacres and race hatred. Otherwise, whole populations and professional classes needed for the reconstruction should have been condemned for supporting the fascist regimes and their deeds in various ways. This, while certainly true, is not sufficient to understand fascism and, above all, to fight it. Fascism is much subtler and more capitalistically banal than its atrocious misdeeds.

Some nostalgic people, and even some non-fascist persons, also remember fascism's efficiency in running traditionally inefficient countries (Italy, Portugal, Spain, various Latin American and Eastern European nations). Such aspect is well rendered by the following quotation from an author who is very important to our purpose here and with whom we will meet time and again: 'Today the trains – not only the international expresses but also the local trains – are punctual to the minute' (Einzig, 1933, p. 21).

The above observation corresponds to a proverbial expression typical of Italians with a sense of nostalgia – *e i treni arrivavano in orario!* [Transl.: and the trains arrived on time!]. Such an attitude to efficiency is revelatory of a much wider ideological position that collapses the political left and right together, well rendered by a statement of the pre-fascist Mussolini that Sternhell (1993) aptly quotes in his useful book:

> La rivoluzione non è il caos, non è il disordine, non è lo sfasciamento di qualsiasi attività, di ogni vincolo della vita sociale,

come opinano gli estremisti idioti di certi paesi; la rivoluzione
ha un senso e una portata storica soltanto quando rappresenta un
ordine superiore, un sistema politico, economico, morale di una
sfera più elevate; altrimenti è la reazione, è la Vandea. La
rivoluzione è una disciplina che si sostituisce ad un'altra disciplina, è una gerarchia che prende il posto di un'altra gerarchia.

Mussolini, 1917

[Transl.: Revolution is not chaos, it is not disorder, it is not
the demolition of all activities, of every bond of social life,
as opined by the idiotic extremists of some countries; revolution has a historical sense and momentum only when it
represents a superior order, a political, economic and moral
system at a more elevated level; otherwise it is reaction, it is
the Vandee. Revolution is a discipline that replaces another
discipline, a hierarchy that replaces another hierarchy.]

Transl. Micocci

This corresponds to the capitalist concept of revolution, and
indeed to all the concepts of capitalism in general that we have
shown in Chapter 2. The relevant question here, however, is:
how many people in the left would agree with it, if they did not
know the name of the author?

In what follows, we are going to outline, from the general
perspective adopted in Chapter 2, what we deem for our purposes
here to be the exemplary features of fascism's ideology, intellectual background and economic strategies, as described by
some fundamental authors. We will see that there is much more
than enough in fascism that fits the present-day political and
economic received wisdom. Following an established historical
practice, we will concentrate mainly, but not solely, on Italian
fascism, for the obvious reason that it is the ancestor of all the
other fascisms. In so doing, we will implicitly avoid the discussion of those excesses of German Nazism (for an obvious
instance) that derived from the personal paranoia of its leader,
Adolf Hitler. This is not to deny that fascism allows such paranoia to be implemented at the policy level. On the contrary, such
discussion is beside our present scope and aim, and rather

obvious both in capitalism in general and in fascism, if what we argue is correct.

Our main field of interest here is the exploration of the meaning of the relevant economic concepts and facts. Because we are studying that from the point of view of the dominant intellectuality of capitalism, what we have called its metaphysics, we have defined capitalism as that mode of production in which metaphysics is so preponderant as to erase the material and the abstract in everyday intercourse. Let us see whether fascism is similar in this respect, despite its claims to be a revolutionary ideology, which was widely discussed in the first phase of fascist life.[1] We should bear in mind, in what follows, that we have noted that, in capitalism – in fascism, too – revolution means subversion as well as reform because it has no meaning whatsoever.

Cassirer (1962) and Merker (2009) are important to us to begin with because they are philosophical authors who locate the origins of fascism, and populism, in present parlance, in the dialectical, Hegelian heritage that swept over Europe in the nineteenth century, never to lose its preponderance to the present. This is perfectly compatible with our theoretical background. While Merker (2009) is more general, and cannot bring himself systematically to use the word fascism (he prefers populism, to adumbrate his addressing also contemporary Italian politics in general and Berlusconi's party in particular), Cassirer (1962) (an incomplete book) is the outcome of his direct knowledge of, and direct opposition to, the fascist phenomenon.

It is precisely Cassirer (ibid.) whom we can use to bridge what we must argue here with what we have presented in Chapter 2 about capitalism. To Cassirer, 'myth' has not disappeared with modernity and with the progress of philosophy. Indeed, philosophers such as Gobineau, Carlyle and Heidegger (to take from his book's three most meaningful examples we need to understand fascism) simply re-propose myth. This only can be done in the framework of a Hegelian, or Hegel-like, mentality: 'No other system has done so much for the preparation of fascism and imperialism as Hegel's doctrine of the state' (p. 273).

The connection between the earthly and the divine are a second aspect at the origins of the mistakes that follow. Although important in general, and well worth a thorough study, this is less important to our purposes here, for reasons of space, above all.

Language plays a paramount role in making intellectual absurdities look politically cosy, logical and normal, as argued in Chapter 2 and, more philosophically and well beyond Cassirer, in Micocci (2002, 2009/2010, 2012 and, above all, 2016). Cassirer distinguishes a 'semantic' language, the purpose of which is to ensure normal, ordinary and rational communication, and a 'mythical' language. This last is meant to convey collective feelings, carrying over concepts, ideas and hopes that would otherwise have no ground, and the origins of which are neither rational nor factual. It is no wonder that mythical language becomes aggressive and, it almost goes without saying, evocative, for it is deprived of any logical soundness and of direct reference to material facts and objects. There is no alternative for its survival: not to perish, it must penetrate the semantic language, endowing it with supposedly collective feelings rooted in a nebulous and unjustified common past.

One can easily see the connection with Hegel's collectivism, well displayed in this latter's theories of the state and of right, which Marx felt a duty fiercely to oppose.[2] One can also easily see that collective feelings are necessarily proselytising in nature, for they must hide their impossible character by looking acceptable on account of being widespread: they repress logical rigour and originality – that is, human individuality. This is well explained in theoretical terms in Merker's (2009) discussion of populism and, naturally and in general, by the metaphysics of capitalism.

Cassirer's hypothesis is, in fact, complementary to that put forward by Merker's discussion of populism (here we witness fashion again, like in D'Eramo's 2013 article), which is made (all translations of Merker are Micocci's) of 'speculative, aprioristic reasoning' that refer to 'the most superficial culture of the age' (2009, p. 5). They lead to 'an absolutised concept of people/folk, aprioristic and above all transformed into myth' (ibid., p. 11). As with Cassirer, Merker looks into the errors of the European philosophical past, mentioning, among others, De Maistre, Mazzini, Gioberti, Schmitt, Heidegger and of course, foremost, Hegel. We cannot escape, as argued in Micocci (2002, 2009/2010, 2012, 2016), a critique of Hegel if we want to build a non-capitalist logic, which Marx attempted, only to be hijacked by the base Hegelianism of his mainstream interpreters. Fascism does the opposite.

Merker and Cassirer are giving their own, limited version of what we have argued in Chapter 2 to be the general historical mentality of capitalism as we know it and of its language. We witness the capitalist metaphysics that permeates and penetrates everything, from actual political and economic intercourses to intellectual endeavours. Only by imposing itself as universal (and as a universal, in Hegelian language) can it lead to the absurdities of capitalist economic relationships and to their justi-fication by economic theories (or, for that matter, to their inef-fectual opposition by mainstream Marxisms). Material things and persons take up a metaphysical meaning, thereby relegating their concrete existence (even emotional) to an accessory attrib-ute – that is, yet another myth. Community, private property, economic value and nation/patriotism are typical examples of absurdities that become true with reference to a nebulous and unspecified past. Populism and fascism are simply using them, with one advantage vis-à-vis other, more pensive economic subjects: they just use it, without thinking about it.

A powerful aid to all this is supplied by the control of impulses and emotions that the metaphysics of capitalism and its language can, and do, perform. Reich, another author unjustly forgotten in our repressive days, in the Preface to the Third Edition (1970) of his book straightforwardly says that fascism:

> is only the organised political expression of the structure of the average man's character, a structure that is ... general and international ... is the basic emotional attitude of the suppressed man of our authoritarian machine civilisation

and its mechanistic-mystical conception of life ... [which] produces fascist parties, and not vice versa.

p. xiii, emphasis in the original

He adds that fascism 'represents an amalgam in between *rebellious* emotions and reactionary social ideals' (p. XIV, emphasis in the original).

There is no room here to discuss in depth Reich's own sexual interpretation of this whole matter, although we would love it, because it would strengthen our point. It is worth noticing, however, that he does not mention Hegel. He limits himself to a criticism of Fromm (p. 219). Certainly, the rebellious yet simultaneously reactionary character of fascism (studied in the same terms by Gentile, 1996, 2005, and Sternhell, 1993) explains very well, besides fascism itself,[3] many contemporary phenomena as well. (For a recent instance, the extension of marriage to minority sexual categories, whose very existence should have instead logically pointed to the absurdity of the institution of marriage[4] itself.)

In other words, the metaphysical (mythical) thinking of capitalism that fascism typically uses and even enhances, without which it could not propose absurdities such as organic society, tradition, corporative solutions to international relations as conflict among nations, nationalism and so on, is the best way to mix up rebellion to injustice with ideas that are banal and common, and even reactionary, in capitalism as we know it. Fascist economic and political proposals appear to be, as a result, simultaneously against capitalism (for they oppose, say, the exploitation of the people by the plutocracy, or imperialism directed at the wrong target – that is, countries nationally organised, or potentially so) and fully favourable to basic capitalist ideas (governments supervising corporatist exploitation, free economic initiative, wealth of nations, fair banking). All this only can happen within the frame of a strong, well-organised state in which class struggle is tamed into class harmony and interaction. How many on the left would disagree with that? How many entrepreneurs, managers and market ideologists of today would subscribe to that?

Gentile (1996, 2005) has had the merit of showing what everybody (take Sweezy, 1962, for a typical Marxist example) had been seeking to hide since the 1930s: fascism not simply had an ideology, it had ideas.[5] Such ideas, as happens all the time for all political parties, were put aside or diluted once in power, while they were much discussed in the earlier, constituent phase. More importantly, however, they were, and are, poor and vague – that is, in the absurdity of the capitalist metaphysics, practical (and feasible and rational, as explained in Micocci, 2016). They look usable, or seem to propose operational things. In fact, as said, the main outcome of the metaphysics of capitalism is that it deprives all things and all reasoning of their ontological connections to reality. Struggle, for a striking example, becomes a metaphysical concept that can, and indeed must, be mentioned, invoked and even blamed all the time, but never practised other than blandly.[6] A quick look at the history of capitalist political struggles of all types easily proves the point. (See Micocci, 2012.)

The above is well conveyed by the umbrella term of 'pragmatism', of which the fascists, as Gentile (2005, 1996) and Sternhell (1993) argue and Einzig (1933) and Bandini (1957) confirm, were masters. Indeed, Gentile (2005, 1996) notes, fascism endowed itself with a set of practical ideas for practical politics – tools for political struggle. It was and is fundamental to this purpose – indeed, for every political force in any political era – to have an internal debate alternating between a polite dialectics and a straightforward clash of ideas. Mussolini's career was characterised by his tolerance for such internal debate until the fake radicalisation entailed by the creation of the Repubblica Sociale, following 8 September 1943. Hitler instead, which explains much of the antipathy he aroused during his lifetime, did not allow that type of conversation: take, for an instance, his way of handling diversity: the night of the long knives episode.

Everything else around this core of pragmatic economic and political ideas was just Cassirer's mythical language, or, in our own terms, an enhanced and overexcited practise of the metaphysics of capitalism. It is only in this light that we can critically understand the role of past thinkers in the creation of fascist ideologies, which further strengthens our contention that such ideas were vague, and even useless to the final purpose of gaining power. Sternhell (1993), for instance, has long discussions on Sorel and on the French reactionary writers, which, while not clashing with Gentile (2005, 1996), are quite inconclusive: how much of Sorel is in fascism? How many fascist leaders read it and actually pondered it? We all can see, however, why and how such thinkers matter, and why fascism would not have existed without them and without Comte, Spencer and many others. But they, too, are myths in Cassirer's sense, obscured by the fascist (and the forces opposing fascism) pragmatism, which is in itself yet another myth in Cassirer's sense.

What has been said so far, however, would not be convincing at the popular level, and hence it would not persuade the economists and the intellectuals, these organic and indispensable high-minded transformers of trivialities into truth, who matter so much when ideas are to become popular (see Micocci, 2016). What are needed to achieve political success with both the intellectuals and the folks are true myths. By this is meant myths that, however absurd or unlikely, look established in their origin, constitute themselves as endless sources of (metaphysical, capitalist) reasoning, and look for feasible (pragmatic) objectives. Nationalism (take the perverted conclusion made in all ages and places between national independence and liberty, and its rendition in 1932 by fascism, in particular, so close to our time), corporatism (often this last is proposed today, hiding its name), order, efficiency, fairness, reduction of economic exploitation, independence, free economic initiative, the market, biological food and what have you are in the pool of ideas from which you can fish: the endless arsenal of capitalist metaphysical stupidities.

The general framework we are presented with at this point is, therefore, simply, the metaphysics of capitalism, with its non-persons, non-objects and its set of theoretical securities about the economy, politics and even nature. There is no hint whatsoever of the possibility of otherness, unless one thinks of the threatened presence of yet other metaphysical myths: the communist anarchist, or any likely substitute of it. This last character is unanimously disliked by everybody, including communists themselves. Its metaphysical avatar in the form of material persons[7] is chased down, arrested and executed by all regimes alike, while the communist anarchist itself (the ideas) remains alive: a ghost, a doubly metaphysical myth that adumbrates the natural man.

No matter how many you eliminate, and even whether any single one of them ever existed, the communist anarchist's threat to capitalist pragmatism is there to stay for fascists, Christians and communists alike and, indeed, for everybody else. It is other from capitalism, but it does not matter because, when it is pronounced other by capitalism it is meant, as we have seen endless times, to be only different. Hence, the cruelty of the treatment meted out to it: the other must be reduced to the diverse, and the only way to do so is by killing it, because 'other' intellectually means incommunicable, while death is universal but can be reduced easily, and paradoxically, to yet another vulgar Hegelian discourse of diversity and mediation. Fascism uses, in other words, the cruelty and repression it finds in capitalist societies.

Capitalism, as well as its reformed fascist version, can only go on delving in capitalist environments. It must pursue the mainstream theories, the mainstream practice and the mainstream devising of economic policies, or it would not be participating in the national and international economic system. It is condemned, to cut a long story short, just as Schmitt proposed (see, for instance, Balakrishnan, 2011; Tesche, 2011; Galli, 2001) to forever defend itself against similarly aimed nations (i.e. organic communities), fascist or not. That is why it must pragmatically refer to the normal (in the statistical sense, as well as in the common sense) items of mainstream economic and political management.

Fascism, inevitably, is not second to anybody in this respect, as Einzig (1933), a British observer and an economist sympathetic to fascism, helps us notice. Italian fascism, he tells us (ibid., pp. 7–9), acknowledges the preponderance of the economic over the political,[8] and the unavoidability of classes, which must necessarily be kept in peace with one another. Private property must, as a consequence, be managed by a corporatist state. Prosperity is axiomatically based on social peace (p. 11), which denies what Adam Smith had to say on the role of class struggle and, naturally, all types of liberal philosophies. One is led to wonder why all present regimes call themselves liberal, therefore, for they all practise corporatism. See Micocci (2016); Di Mario and Micocci (in preparation); Di Mario (2015).

Einzig goes on to define fascist corporatism as the means to reach such social efficiency, while he wonders (1933, p. 27) whether the ultimate aims of fascism are far from clear. In any case, it is urgent, and just obvious because it is everybody's concern in capitalism, to manage and harmonise individual and collective interest (p. 84, among others). Banks must be controlled, but their managers must not feel protected by the state, lest they undertake imprudent operations (pp. 82–9, 95), which means that the nature of banks in fascism remains the same as in non-fascist countries. While private initiative is natural (another myth present-day economists would not hesitate to endorse immediately), monopolies, cartels and trusts are to be avoided. Production must nonetheless remain in private hands (p. 35), while wages must be 'elastic' (p. 39). The government intervenes in production only when private initiative fails.[9]

In sum, to Einzig there is a common interest between labour and capital, and industrial peace can and must be pursued at the price of reducing political freedom (p. 65). The point (p. 69) is not to have equal shares, but to raise everybody's lot by increasing output. Now that we are saying it here, it sounds universal, and hence banal. But it does not when it is uttered in a fascist or neoliberal setting.

From the monetary point of view, Mussolini's policy has been 'strictly orthodox' (p. 78), despite the hope Einzig shares with the fascists of a 'relaxation' of the strictness of the rules in the distant future (p. 82).[10] All this requires the instillation of a sense of duty in the population: patriotism can solve that problem easily (pp. 99–100). We should again see this in the light of the fascist idea popularised then and now by Schmitt (see Balakrishnan, 2011; Tesche, 2011; Galli, 2001) that international relations are made of (vulgar Hegelian) conflicts with the ensuing temporary supremacies. The enduring popularity of Schmitt today testifies to the banality of such an idea in the metaphysics of capitalism.

If laissez faire were replaced by fascism in all countries, Einzig argues that the dangers and pitfalls of the international system would be lessened (1933, pp. 105–6). The true interdependence of nations would be apparent. In fact (p. 107), Einzig has no doubt that fascism and socialism are very similar. Planning is important in order to avert crises (p. 117). Fascism might well live for ever (pp. 120–1), especially when it is in the 'capable hands' of men as great (!) as Mussolini and Salazar. Let Einzig speak on the most important issue, however:

> The conception that an increase of state intervention is an inevitable necessity is gaining ground in every country. In Great Britain it has adherents in every political party ... Without any spectacular change in the political regime, an economic system approaching fascism may then be introduced, if not in form, at any rate in substance .... unlike Communism, the Corporate system is elastic and adaptable.
>
> Ibid., p. 122

In Japan it would be easy to adopt it, thanks to the patriotism of the population and of the regime.

> It is even conceivable ... that ... in the United States a system will emerge which economically will not be very far from fascism. The firm hand with which President Roosevelt deals with big business seems to point in that direction.
>
> Ibid.

The policies of privatisation Bel (2006, 2011) discusses for fascist Italy and Nazi Germany should, as a consequence, not amaze us in any way. Bel shows their rationale to be multiple, and not just the (obvious) need to please those powerful classes that had helped fascism come about or had been initially suspicious of it and had to be lured to it. This is the consequence of the necessity, for parties and ideologies that identify themselves with only the petty bourgeois (especially in mentality, Reich 1970 reminds us), to reach a universal consensus in the economic – that is, capitalistic, management of the country, as confirmed by most authors. It suffices to mention here Bandini (1957) because its narrow focus on agricultural economics leads him to the very same conclusions as most others: fascist economic policies were eclectic – that is, vague and practical in the sense we have argued in Chapter 2.

We should never forget that fascism historically also gave Italy IRI (Istituto Ricostruzione Industriale), on which the post-war boom and planning were built, and a modern and up to date capitalist Central Bank (*Banca d'Italia*). The capitalist modernisation of the whole country is greatly indebted to them. *A posteriori* one can attribute this or that rationale to such decisions. We are stating here instead that, whatever the rationale, such actions were simply inevitable in the metaphysics of capitalism. They can be explained with (reformed) mainstream ideas.

As a consequence of all we have said so far, one can explain and study neoliberal ideas through the vulgar Hegelian character of the metaphysics of capitalism, which is the same as that of fascism. There is no room here to host such discussion, which can be found in Micocci (2012, 2016). Rather, it is instructive to notice once again that the vulgarly Hegelian character of the whole thing is not denied by the left and the Marxists, and it seems, surprisingly, not to constitute any problem for them. For one typical and striking example, the Marxist journal *Historical Materialism* has published Schmitt (2014), which comes down to an endorsement of Marx's supposed Hegelianism (non-existent to the present authors and to those who read Marx for what he wrote and not for what the Marxists say he wrote) without a word of criticism and, above all, without seeing the disquieting absurdity of the whole operation (see Micocci, 2016). We should pay closer attention to these things.

We can now finally mention the popularity of fascism by referring the reader to the works of Rosenberg (1934/2012) and Pellicani (2012), who express this disturbing aspect in the most appropriate way, in our view. Fascism was, and is, a mass phenomenon and, at this point, we may easily see why.

In order to continue our discourse on the eclectic ideological nature of fascism and its responding to the needs of capitalism, we turn now to another exemplary instance: Scarpari (2004) writes about the racist elements of Italian fascism who gathered around the racist juridical journal *Il Diritto Razzista* (*Racist Jurisprudence*), helped by the Nazis. The people who willingly collaborated with the Nazis were taken after the war as cadres in the most important Italian institutions. The point is, even accepting the pragmatic principle that you have to use fascist personnel for the reconstruction, why choose those few who had proved, unlike most others, openly racist even after 1943, when fascism appeared doomed? How can one tell fascist racism from everyday, common, democratic racism?

It is worth considering further the following point, which also reconnects us with the discussion of Chapter 2. Ascherson (2016) aptly notes that most biographers of Hitler agree that, in Germany, there was, at all levels, a generalised striving to second-guess and anticipate Hitler, despite his 'absolute and monocratic' regime, which greatly helped practical efficiency in decision-making and policy-making and implementation. The presence of a common mentality that does not break with general economic ideas, whatever they are, as long as they do not threaten the received wisdom, is the same in Nazism as in capitalism in general. Let us then meditate upon the quotation he gives on p. 23, in the knowledge that, as Ascherson notices, most biographers of Hitler see it as typical of the atmosphere of the times. A senior Nazi civil servant, Werner Willikens, in February 1934 thus harangues agricultural officers from all over the Reich: 'The Führer finds it very difficult to bring about by order from above things which he intends to realise sooner or later.' It was, therefore, 'the duty of each one of us to work towards him in the spirit of the Führer [im Sinne des Fürherihen entgegenzarbeiten]'. We invite the reader to replace the rhetoric of the Fürher with that of economic growth, or of the resistance to the sacrifices induced by the crisis, or to the threat of external enemies, or the struggle against terrorism, the immigrants and similar.

Before attempting a telling summary, it is useful to extend to fascism a recent discussion (2015) Wrenn proposes as valid for neoliberalism and capitalism in general. She argues that, in neoliberalism, a 'false consciousness' is created based upon the preaching of individualism. Hard work becomes a 'non-authentic agency', making everybody contribute to the common good by interpreting what must and can be done within the directives power proposes. The individual 'perceives' him/herself to be authentic, while he/she is only part of a big, homogeneous machine. This corresponds, with a different method and language, to what we have outlined respecting the metaphysics of capitalism, and, again – with a different method and language – fascism at the international level. Certainly, it is not what Smith (1999, 2009) intended as free initiative and as the wealth of nations; even less what the liberal philosophers intended as individual freedom (Micocci, 2012; Di Mario and Micocci, in preparation).

It is very instructive, in order to draw some provisional conclusions, to summarise what fascism is all about by means of Galli (2001), which, despite not being a specific book (it is a university instruction book), has the great merit of identifying, among the Italian currents of political thought, a dialectical stream to which Croce and Gramsci, among others, significantly belong and which we have repeatedly indicted here as accomplices to fascism. Despite the difference in language, we would like the reader to compare what we say here to the summary appended at the end of Chapter 2 on capitalism in general.

To Galli (ibid.), the starting point to understand fascism is its belief in the inadequacy of reason, which makes whatever programme/ideology proposed, however ideologically suggestive, hopelessly vague and approximate. There follows a need for practical actions of creation and, again, we find ourselves necessarily dealing with heterogeneity and incoherence. The obvious tool to hold all this together is recurring to supposedly common ideals and ancestors expressed through the mythical language: nation, struggle against injustice (of any kind, comprising, therefore, the immigrants and the Jews). The state thus ends up being the supreme entity, which is no surprise, for fascism fishes from the only common reason Europe has had to posit an organic community: nationalism.

The issue of traditionalism need not be posed, in that both a traditionalist and an anti-traditionalist position are allowed.[11] To be as incoherent as that, the best tool to be efficient is to let a leader interpret the true needs and wants of 'the people', whose thoughts are in tune when society is organic and has a supreme exegete. Hence, the mass party character is easily connected to the overseeing role of the state. In fact, to the philosopher Gentile and to Mussolini (1935), the democratic principle is counteracted only by a 'natural inequality', which makes universal suffrage useless.

That is why Italian fascism (and other fascisms, take Peron's Argentina as a typical instance) could be, at the beginning, both progressive and revolutionary in the capitalist sense of Chapter 2, initially proposing, for instance for Italy, universal franchise, proportional representation, eight hours' work time, minimum wage, etc., and, in 1932, could transform itself, with Gentile's and Mussolini's *La Dottrina del Fascismo* (1935), into a non-democratic regime that celebrated 'natural inequality' and refused universal franchise (just to keep to these two telling instances). After all, the state represents the universal critical will of everybody (the people, the nation, the community, the group) who holds a (the) common ethics (though debates are allowed, as Schmitt made clear when saying that order and disorder must be together, and the former must rule the latter).

The masses are fully integrated in political life, creating a 'democrazia organizzata, centralizzata, autoritaria' (an organised, centralised, authoritarian democracy) (Galli, 2001, p. 406). Corporatism follows suit, for it stems from the reactionary literature – Sorel and Christian (Catholic) social doctrine –

which are part of fascism's historical background. Needless to say, all this can only happen if private economic initiative is free to develop man's 'creativity'. The premises of human homogeneity required by microeconomics are, as a consequence, all there.

Anybody can see the sad similarities with capitalism in general. Indeed, we are talking about the same thing. Let us see whether there are any relevant differences with present-day neoliberalism.

Notes

1 See e.g. Gentile, 2005, 1996; Sternhell, 1993. This was explained but also almost completely denied in 1932 in '*La Dottrina del Fascismo*' (1935), a piece jointly written by Mussolini and Gentile but signed only by the former, and reiterated in a worsened form after 8 September 1943 in the so-called *Manifesto di Verona* of the reconstituted National Party.
2 See Marx's Critique of Hegel's Theory of State, 1845, and Contribution to the Critique of Hegel's Philosophy of Right, 1843–4, both in Marx, 1992. See also Micocci, 2009/2010, 2012, 2016.
3 The most evident and remorseless merger of reactionary ideals and rebelliousness is Franco's varied and reactionary brand of fascism in Spain.
4 This is just a recent and fashionable example. The thing is general: take, as identical instances, TV advertisements, which invite you, or pretend, to 'break the rules' or to 'set new rules', or to 'make your own rules', or even to 'rebel' and 'make oneself independent' or 'creatively enjoy' – cars, mobile communication, hairdo substances, clothing and, most representatively, banking. What you do by breaking the rules is follow them, of course.
5 Bearing in mind what ideas mean in the metaphysics of capitalism.
6 One should not confuse the enormity of fascist misdeeds with the blandness of their intellectual nature. For the cruelty of moderation, see Micocci (2012).
7 In a typical capitalist paradox, where a number of apparent inversions are operated to remain in the end with the same old item, the myth itself. Never mind the physical bodies of people.
8 One must intend it in Einzig's mainstream sense. In fact, if everything argued so far is true, fascism posits that politics is above the economic, even historically, thus marking, luckily, a fundamental difference with Marxism.

9 This is a terribly Hegelian statement all mainstream and Marxist economists, sadly, put forward sooner or later.
10 Is this different from today?
11 Again, look at the analogy today with the legalisation of marriage for sexual minorities, which looks anti-traditionalist while being, inevitably, traditionalist and reactionary.

4 Neoliberalism

There is a great deal of difference between what is called neoliberalism today and its supposed historical origins, which feeds confusion and useless debating. In our present day, by neoliberalism is meant a set of extremely heterogeneous policies discussed, and most of the time implemented, by the vast majority of world governments, regardless of their formal political stance. The EU, the WB and the IMF preside over this set of rites, stamping it with their seal of approval and giving it the value of example and the endorsement of authenticity. The mass media and the intellectuals discuss all the issues involved, but only in technical terms, while the left does the same, adding to it the count of the damage wreaked (see e.g. Harvey, 2005) and formal consternation. A rigorous definition is, therefore, not only useless, but also counter-productive.

In practical terms, neoliberalism monopolises the discussion of economic issues, and there is, therefore, no room for alternatives, nor is any possibility of an alternative even envisaged. The best way to summarise the situation is by the Italian and French expressions *'pensiero unico'/'pensee unique'*: everybody talks about something in terms of that thing only. Some people, however, transport the meaning of this expression to signify a socially dominant thought. The former meaning is the right one. The latter, instead, is what we have named metaphysics, or, more narrowly, mythical thought. A socially dominant thought would mean, in fact, that most people, by joining a *pensee unique*, are simply stupid and also could be – as a consequence – easily cured. It instead represents something that people endorse in their belief and thus represents the ineluctable idea of public opinion, against which they can do nothing. Grossi (2011), among others, has put it perfectly.

The most useful way to succinctly summarise the varied set of policies and the entailed media and political (perfunctory and useless) debate is constituted by the ten sources of neoliberal activity presented by Callinicos (2003), who himself refers to Williamson's (1990) famous definition. Neoliberalism proposes to work, for its dream of free market,[1] on ten nebulous points: fiscal discipline, public expenditure, fiscal reform, financial liberalisation, competitive exchange rates, liberalisation of trade, foreign direct investment, privatisation, deregulation, property rights. Even a cursory look at the mentioned list, nonetheless, makes one notice that the capitalist elites are going to benefit from the liberalisations proposed.[2] Some, especially in the left media, tend to think that this is a deliberate class struggle move.

More importantly, however, this quasi-utopian[3] character of neoliberalism needs, in order to be implemented, a state that is not only capable of intervening in the economy directly and without qualms. It also needs a strong state apparatus that controls and represses, first, the sufferings and, then, the protests and riots that are inevitably bound to crop up when the inequality gap is enhanced and the industrial base (material production) is destroyed; neoliberal policies, in fact, as signalled in Chapter 2, tend to resolve themselves in the financialisation of the economy (the M-M' circuit) (see Micocci, 2016; Gallino, 2011; Dore, 2009). To achieve this result, the state must present itself as the interpreter of a coherent connection between an organic popular basis that collectively strives to increase wealth and the pragmatic issues that the economy and international needs dictate. This is, as we saw, a fascist goal.

Governance and all the other catchwords that are proposed can thus be interpreted as a new vocabulary for old concepts. Indeed, as Moretti and Pestre (2015) show for the very important case of the World Bank, language has shifted from reference to the material objects of economics, the interaction of states, the Bank and the rest, to reference to immaterial objectives/metaphysical[4] concepts to do with 'management'. Opportunities, challenges, agendas, strategies bring to an end the old-style surveys and reports, to the coming of 'focusing, strengthening and implementing, monitor, control, audit, indicators, expertise, effectiveness, efficiency, performance, competitiveness and innovation' (ibid., p. 80). Governance is, inevitably, the dominant word. When we look into them, we can see the modern version of slogans and catchwords of the fascist era. Some terms (but not the concepts underlying them)[5] are new for obvious historical reasons – as for the terms related to information technologies (IT), for example – but most can be traced back to the fascist era, or to more recent fascisms such as Argentina under Peron and its recent Peronist leaders (another thing the left mistakenly looks at with sympathy far too often).

Despite all this vagueness and internal freedom to act, it is worth recalling at this point that 'neoliberalism' as a term was coined in the late 1930s (Mirowski and Plehwe, 2009),[6] when a theoretical formula to avoid the recurrence of economic crisis of the early 1930s was needed. The group of liberal intellectuals gathered in Paris for the Walter Lippmann Colloquium established it with the intent to renew liberalism by rejecting the old laissez faire to avoid the failures of capitalism, collectivism and socialism. The unanimous consent of the early neoliberal intellectuals was to put together two ideas: create a new liberal project and reject the failures and pitfalls of capitalism,[7] similarly to Einzig, as we saw in an earlier chapter.

The agreement on the core concepts of the theoretical proposal was poor due to the predictable antagonism between the traditionalists and the innovators who did not agree on the role of the state and how this last relates to society. Rüstow and Lippmann proposed a strong state supervision, while the group of Mises and Hayek supported the abolishment of barriers to market entry as the only legitimate role for the state (ibid.). This early disagreement would later prove useful, for it allowed neoliberalism to take the different forms in practise than those to which we have already alluded.

The Walter Lippmann Colloquium was essentially replaced with the foundation of the Mont Pelerin Society (ibid.; Mirowski, 2013, still sees in this society the roots of the present evil) in 1947, in which Hayek brought together believers in the free market, classical liberal and neoliberal intellectuals and political figures. In his 1944 *The Road to Serfdom* (a commendable anti-fascist bible, adding contradiction to contradiction), Hayek (2001) famously argued that economic control is not merely control of a sector of human life that can be separated from the rest; it is the control of the means for all our ends.

After the 1960s, the term 'neoliberal' declined and was later revived in the 1980s in connection with Augusto Pinochet's economic reforms in Chile. The definition and usage of the term has changed over time. However, neoliberalism constantly claims, in order to promote a free market economy, to refer to theories of laissez faire from classical liberalism. The term became common in the 1970s and 1980s due to the resurgence of ideas associated with laissez faire, economic liberalism, free trade, de-regulation, privatisation, fiscal austerity and the dismantling of the welfare benefits that concentrated upon the areas summarised in Callinicos's ten points proposed at the beginning of the present chapter. Monetarism, supply-side economics, Lucas's and Buchanan's critiques of economic policing and their evolutions represented the basic economic theory, which they could use as a start.

The late neoliberal intellectuals notoriously drove everybody's attention away from the issue of what the state should do for economics and society to what economics can do for society with the help of the state. Friedman (1962) conceptualised economic freedom as an extremely important component of total freedom, for it constitutes a necessary condition for political freedom. Scholars such as Mirowski (2009, 2013) currently tend reductively to correlate neoliberalism, as discussed above, with the theories of Friedrich Hayek and Milton Friedman. Here we witness a blatant case of mythical language in Cassirer's (1962) sense.

Being, however, historically related today – helped by the inordinate influence of the mass media comprising the internet – to the economic policies introduced by Margaret Thatcher in the United Kingdom, Ronald Reagan in the United States and Pinochet in Chile, neoliberalism is commonly associated with neo-conservatism and austerity, the so-called Washington Consensus, free market/market-oriented policies, supply-side economics, rational expectations and monetarism. This economic and political pliability and variety makes neoliberalism both easy to use and hard to pin down.[8]

The misty nature of neoliberalism resides in this commonly accepted and simplified understanding of the neoliberal state. In this politically and economically controversial terrain, economics meets politics, starting with the assumption that the neoliberal knowledge of socio-economic dynamics is cognitively superior because it applies the scientific indicators (already spelt out in their effects in Chapter 2) of efficiency, efficacy and equity, which are market fascistic features. An important question stems from the above, however: if economic enterprises, agents and individuals are truly market-oriented believers and practitioners of the self-regulated free markets and are able to put into practise efficiency and efficacy regardless of the political contexts, why do neoliberals' interests address all spheres of societies worldwide and deal with equity and political regimes?

As a partial and temporary conclusion to what has so far been said, we can argue that, while the origins and nature of neoliberalism as a doctrine or school of thought are fairly clear, its scientific and technical coherence are undermined by the lack in mainstream scholarship, to which they necessarily must refer, of a common vision of the role of the state and of organisation. This problem, which, as said, created in the past a controversy between traditionalists (Hayek and Mises) and innovators (Lippman and Rüstow), later on proved, on the contrary, to be a practical solution and indeed an opportunity for neoliberal policies to avoid moral constraints on the use of power, thus accepting any political set-up, whether democratic or reactionary, to fulfil the project of a market-oriented society.

Despite the fact that 'liberal' thinkers generally seem to prefer to express 'liberal' opinions and publicly manifest humanism rather than reactionary beliefs and brutalism, the Popperian 'good face' of the 'open society' is not necessarily a requisite of the neoliberal project, but rather a matter left to the religion, moral constituency and good manners of the neoliberal individual, and the immeasurable influence of the mass media. This does not facilitate those critics who see neoliberalism and democracy as contradictory or incompatible. They (the 'liberals') should explain the pervasiveness and coexistence of neoliberal policies with both authoritarian and democratic regimes, which they cannot, for lack of theoretical ground. Here lie the roots of the present-day difficulties in assessing neoliberalism, or of choosing terms such as 'populism' and the like to represent it. Hence, the easiness with which it has spread.

The expansion of neoliberal ideology cannot, in other words, be explained only in terms of the adaptability of an economic praxis to become a holistic tool to approach life, but also to its ability to homogenise the composite dimensions of a societal structure by pretending to be individually based. Since its foundation, neoliberalism has shown a great ability to be employed in various political contexts because it can wave its mainstream political, moral and economic centrality. It can be identified with a 'capability to restructure' economic, political and social systems, regardless of the starting conditions, because of its homogenising, unilateral and mythical attitude in conducting economics and society towards a neoliberal trajectory[9], which, after all, is a quasi-utopia: a pseudo-liberal, or market, trajectory. Whether there is the presence of a dictator or of a democratic regime, neoliberal actions can be adopted by executing them under new rules that pretend to be, as we shall show in the next chapter, self-explanatory. We can take as examples the dictatorship of Pinochet in Chile and the Bush administrations in the USA for their linkages between neoliberal academic activism, adoption of neoliberal policies and human repression at home and abroad.

Springer, in a form that is approximately and at first sight similar and complementary to what we are seeking to do here, considers neoliberalism 'an ideological construct' (Springer, 2010) and a discourse through which a political economic form of power-knowledge is constructed (Springer, 2012): 'Neoliberalism is a pure, paradigmatic, and static construct of universal, monolithic, and exogenous processes that transforms places from somewhere "outside," resulting always and everywhere in the same homogenous [sic] and singular outcome as the sequencing is predefined' (Springer, 2014, p. 3). In Springer's view, 'neoliberalism' as a term can be conceived as a noun or a verb with different consequences:

> The idea that neoliberalism itself is 'in crisis' presupposes an understanding of neoliberalism in the sense of a noun. That is, the designation of 'ism' leads us to a dead end inasmuch as it represents a theoretical abstraction that is disconnected from actual experience ...
>
> In utilizing this dynamic conception of neoliberalism-as-a-*verb* over static notions of neoliberalism-as-a-*noun* we arrive at the conclusion that while particular social spaces, regulatory networks, sectoral fields, local formations, and so forth will frequently be hampered by crises, this does not necessarily imply that they will resonate throughout an entire aggregation of neoliberalism. In other words, because 'neoliberalism' indeed does not exist as a coherent and fixed edifice, as an equilibrium complex, or as a finite end-state, it is consequently unlikely to fail in a totalizing moment of collapse (Peck *et al.* 2010).
>
> Springer, 2014, p. 3, emphasis in the original

The above is historically relevant and fundamental for us here. In relation to the 2007/8 crisis that still is with us, Palma (2009) adds, in a special issue of the *Cambridge Journal of Economics* dedicated to the subject, that:

> neoliberalism is not a set of economic policies but a new and more effective technology of power ... the capitalist elite, mainly because of lack of credible opposition and its intrinsic rentier nature, instead of using this new technology of power for its intended 'rationalising' effects, ended up misusing it to support more effective forms of dispossession and more

rentier forms of accumulation. This has transformed capitalism into a ('sub-prime') system with little capacity to develop the productive forces of society – i.e., one that has lost its only historical legitimacy.

Ibid., p. 847

The ideological component of neoliberal capitalism is clearly identifiable (and yet invisible, untouchable, vague and precise, simultaneously) as it manifests itself in an active discipline within the power centres of the state and a social institution, and is used to legitimise the theory and practise of Palma's 'class of rentiers', the elite of bureaucrats and/or the financial speculators.[10]

Ideology in the common area between academic and productive contexts is used as a veil to create consensus, to express the neoliberal predicaments, and to cover the neoliberal incoherence at the theoretical and practical levels. The mass media and all those who practise *pensee unique* connive. The ideological component materialises in specific neoliberal constructs. For a couple of powerful examples, we can consider the neoliberal reinterpretation of Adam Smith's invisible hand (Di Mario and Micocci, 2015, in preparation), as well as, for instance, the practical policies or actions such as the so-called Bottom of the Pyramid (BOP) (Karnali, 2009). The neoliberal ideology works through neoliberal agents who, as we shall see, distort and, above all, limit language and logic to then use them for implementing pseudo-academic and managerial approaches, managing consent and control, building corporatism.

Part of the explanation must be sought in the passage from an industrial to a post-Fordist production and organisation of work, which occurred with the 1970s crisis. This has changed structures and roles in the dynamics between capital and labour with the result of a shift of income away from labour and a reaction to social movements (Harvey, 1989), with insecurity and uncertainty being introduced (Bourdieu, 1998; Standing, 2011; Fleming, 2015). One can see neoliberalism as based on the methodical domination of labour by capital. Human geographer

Harvey, from his mainstream Marxist perspective, also described neoliberalism as a class project, designed to impose one class on society through liberalism (Harvey, 2005). Indeed, Harvey explains neoliberalism in terms of a type of class restoration operated by capitalists, specifically rentier capitalists, operating in the wake of the 1970s crisis, which expresses itself at the theoretical level by proposing an international capitalist system and, at the practical level, by re-establishing the accumulation process for a class of elites (ibid.). Here comes the need for neoliberalism to activate management as a rational function of capitalist production, spreading its principles from the economic sector to the rest of the non-economic sectors of society by an impetus provided by managerialism itself. We shall come back to such complications in the next chapter.

The latter case portrays what happened during the 2008 crisis and the current state of capitalism, which Gallino identifies with his '*finanzcapitalism*' neologism (Gallino, 2011). Financial rentiers impose their free finance market regimes by ideological domination in the equivocal, mediating sense we have mentioned already so many times, in which no one seems to be fully right or wrong. Later, the socio-economic path of restructuring materialises by the payment of financial debts with public resources and the austerity plans, which together increase the distrust towards institutions. Very little of the theoretical apparatus is used in all this.

Palma (2009) shows how the increased process of 'financialisation' led to a remarkable decoupling between the real and financial worlds. This is fundamental for us here, as stated from the beginning.

During the period of so-called 'financial repression' that followed the Bretton Woods agreement in 1944, total financial assets remained relatively stable as a share of GDP for about three decades (at a level of about 500%), while private investment experienced some acceleration (the two extreme points in the cycle were 13.8% of GDP in 1961 and 18.5% in 1979). The subsequent period of 'financial liberalisation', a period of huge asset inflation (that more than doubled the value of total financial assets as a share of GDP) was accompanied by a slowdown of the rate of private investment (from 18.5% of GDP in 1979 to 15.5% in 2007).

During this period the value of financial assets not only decoupled from the real economy, but the abundance of finance and the associated asset-price-led (not so) 'irrational exuberance', instead of having a positive pulling effect on private investment, had the negative effect of 'friendly fire'.

Ibid., pp. 40–1

The apparent paradox of a higher profit for non-productive activities, which, instead, we have seen to be a most coherent development of the intellectual logics of capitalism (the metaphysics) and within it of the logic of profits is at the base of Gallino's *finanzcapitalism*, also enhances the pervasiveness of the metaphysics of capitalism. The creation of an invisible and intangible world of assets, which include financial products but also licences and patents and their preponderance in the neoliberal system, reveals itself as a metaphysics to the naked eye. A thorough quotation is, therefore, in order, to show in practice what we have argued in theory above:

The very concept of metaphysics implies the construction of a general framework that puts in place the various subjects and forces of the system that is being analysed. Indeed, the negative connotation of metaphysics in our time comes from its presumption of being able to organise what is behind what is visible, at the risk of abusing reality by bestowing on it a logic that is not necessarily its own. The capitalist metaphysics does this by construing an intermediate rational system, suspended in between the material (the concrete) and the abstract (pure thought constrained only by logical needs).

Micocci, 2016, p. 17

We can argue, by looking at reality, that 'the intermediate rational system' created by the neoliberal capitalist metaphysics contains very little or no theory but has an avatar in the fascist 'rationale' of the revolution as 'order' or, better said, as a superior order (*'ordine superiore'*) managed by a 'superior' neoliberal intellectuality and a 'discipline' or a 'hierarchy' that can be replaced at will and forever by another, similar object. This last fundamental similarity adds up to the other we have shown so far. We will continue to identify similarities in the way the fascist and neoliberal ideology are conceived, and their manifestation. Neoliberalism appears as the best interpreter of the nature of the capitalist metaphysics as it evolves and regenerates itself with apparently new and distinctive features. The most important is the unjustified belief that neoliberal ideas can manage both the economic and social dimensions of human life and make a healthier society for all: a peculiar, among the many possible, use of Cassirer's 'myth'. In order to apply neoliberalism in a pervasive mode, the neoliberal recipes, as said, range from old neoclassical scholarship to fashion style neoliberal pro-poor.

Neoliberal scholarship without caution pretends to date back all the way to 1776, the year of Adam Smith's *Wealth of Nations*, obviously referring to the international tradition of that basic classical political economist, but it went on by continuous misinterpretations of Smith's metaphor of the invisible hand.[11] This is a common mistake of all mainstream-based neoliberal approaches (Di Mario and Micocci, 2015, in preparation). Then there is the bold so-called BOP, a neoliberal pro-poor proposal that continues to chop the money of the poor, pretending to help them with economic and charitable formulas regardless of their misery through the UN system, mainstream NGOs and all the predator charities included in the BOP. Recently *The Economist* criticised the BOP for the assumption that the poor must maximise their utility preferences, which are congruent with their true self-interest. Indeed, the hypothesis of the BOP is not confirmed by empirical evidence because it is an ideological assumption in favour of the free market and of neoliberal policies (see also Karnali, 2009). In the Third World, exploitation of raw materials and the transferral of material production are accompanied by active neoliberal policies towards the orientation and determination of consumption and production, which are similarly imposed through the mythical language of 'the regulating power of the market' turned into 'the self-regulating power of the consumers'.

There is also the fact that the market is unruly with respect to any attempt to make it ordered in any policy sense, which is mistaken in mainstream economics by stating that the market is an unpredictable thing (only in the eyes of the capitalist beholder; see Di Mario and Micocci, 2015, in preparation). This is seen, nonetheless, as a lighthouse for capitalist/managerial orientations, for it creates an apparent substantial instability of economics and of the economy that pushes capital to search for profits outside the corporate interests. Schipper (2011, p. 1) argues that neoliberalism is:

> a qualitative alteration of liberal governmentality along two different, but interrelated movements: Market and competition are, first, no longer represented as natural and self-sustaining outcomes, but as mechanisms, which have to be protected and cared-for by the state. Furthermore, market and competition mentalities are no more limited to what traditionally appeared to be the economy, but that all social relations should be subjected and reorganised in a way that makes markets and competition work.

Due to the recurrent capitalistic crises, the difficulties in understanding the economic cycle, the corporate business and strategy incoherence (Hyman, 1987), neoliberals have come to pay attention to non-profit areas. Social responsibility (just for another item of fashion) has thus entered the neoliberal domain, renamed and made dominantly known through its 'corporate social responsibility' version. Similar things have happened to welfare and corporate welfare. Neoliberalism has been able to generate a role for ethics and even a business ethics as an extreme and tireless producer of economic and 'social' policies. The pretentious ambition of neoliberalism to be superiorly correct is evidently fascist.

Domestic and international brutalities are a characterising factor of neoliberalism, as a result of using moderation and the

ensuing pragmatism of intolerance for both diversity and otherness and for alternatives to the neoliberal capitalistic model,
against any dynamic that can potentially subvert the neoliberal
project (see Micocci, 2012, and the preceding chapters). In this
sense, neoliberal brutalities and intolerance to alternative
perspectives are ontologically similar to fascist brutalities. It
is all a banally capitalist, vulgar Hegelian matter, however
(Micocci, 2016).

It appears clearly from what has been said so far that neoliberalism is but 'capitalism as we know it' without its cultural
debates, and as such it is akin to fascist (lack of) ideas about
politics, economy and society, as argued in Chapter 3. It manifests itself with horror towards forms of sociality that are not
based on the standard capitalist state, and on the perception of
the 'other' as either a threat or an ally (that is, as usual, because
otherness is disregarded and is replaced with diversity). Take, as
a graphic example, city militarism, the trend to militarise cities
to protect neoliberal targets (see, for instance, Coleman, 2004)
and neoliberal institutions and whoever acts in their name (see
Potter, 2015). Such militaristic tendency escalates with the
excuse of international terrorism. 'Different races' or creeds are
seen as a threat to the unilateralism of the societal neoliberal
model in the forms of 'racially driven Neoliberalism and
Neoliberally fuelled racisms' (e.g. Goldberg, 2009, p. 337),
which perfectly match with the fascist social practices of repression and of the representation of the other as to be subjected,
oppressed, marginalised and, hopefully, eliminated.

More generally,[12] the old (capitalist or not) vice of militarism
masqueraded as neoliberal discipline and rationalism expresses
itself in police violence and mass incarceration (Wacquant,
2009, 2012). In Italy (*Il manifesto*, 17 March 2017), common
crime has gone down in the last year by 9.4 per cent, but the
'perception' of crime, so the politicians claim, has paradoxically
increased, thus rendering vain that result. (See also Micocci,
2016.) Wacquant (2009) goes as far as to argue that, in advanced
capitalistic societies, the marginalisation of the poor is turned
into incrimination and punishment through mass incarceration.
The penalisation of poverty appears as a neoliberal way to

manage the effect of its disruptive policies at the lower end of the social structure. Brutality is expressed today with particular emphasis on the most vulnerable groups as a form of violence against the poor through economic aggression and elimination. We could continue with an endless number of examples to enlighten the reader. There is almost no need at this point to emphasise instead (to shorten our story) that neoliberalism has not brought anything new into the way capitalism behaves. As a consequence, it has not diminished or changed in any way the fascist features of capitalism as we know it. On the contrary, it has enhanced the capacity this last has to organise in practice, and simplify in theory, the characteristics of the metaphysics of capitalism. Interestingly, everybody has lost sight of the free market in theory and practise, and economic theory is either not considered or taken for granted and taught only in its mainstream, dominant version.

As shown throughout this chapter, neoliberalism achieves all that is being described here by creating its own power made of metaphysics and language. The combination of a fictitious world thus created and made definitive by 'scientific' analyses, and the alterations this brings to reality and the sense of an enhanced anxiety (Micocci and Di Mario, in preparation) due to the misunderstanding of risk and uncertainty, needs a specialised militia to manage it. This last is supplied by another myth à la Cassirer: managerialism and the managers themselves.

The Marxist Sweezy (1962) reviewed a book by Burnham that made a lot of noise at the time (Burnham, 1942).[13] In it, the ex-Trotzkyst Burnham claimed that managerialism would gain enough independence as to condition the life of nations. He claimed that Nazi Germany, the USSR and the New Deal were examples, at different levels, of this tendency. The managerial class will determine economic life similarly, but long before the neoliberal (and often mainstream) claim that the management of the state and that of the firms are alike.[14] We shall see how all this has developed in capitalism as we know it in what comes next.

Notes

1 Itself, again, a typical myth à la Cassirer due to its impossible definition, pursuance and implementation. See Micocci, 2016.

2 Even if it were not, which is entirely possible, its results are not, to neoliberal eyes, as disastrous as the left pretends. We should not forget, in this respect, that the neoliberal eyes are also the eyes of the common people, rich and poor, who have voted into power the neoliberal parties. In fact, from a neoliberal point of view, inequality is conducive to a quasi-Smithian version of the invisible hand (see Micocci, 2016, and Di Mario and Micocci, 2015 for a critique of this mistake) and therefore to welfare. Voters do understand this, and they seem to like it.

3 Here by quasi-utopian is meant what is explained in Chapter 2 and Micocci (2016).

4 Their use of the word 'metaphysics' is different from ours here, but this discussion is fairly unimportant at this point. They mean metaphysics in the common usage.

5 It is worth reminding the reader that, in the metaphysics of capitalism, the material nature of objects simply does not matter.

6 Which obviously helped its being distinguished from fascism in technical and common parlance, as hinted at the beginning of Chapter 3.

7 This was supposed to be pursued with the foundation of a permanent think tank called 'Centre International d'Études pour la Rénovation du Libéralisme' (Mirowski and Plehwe, 2009).

8 In his *Capitalism and Freedom* (1962), Friedman commented that centralised control of economic activities was always accompanied by political repression. Some of Friedman's followers argue that increasing economic freedoms tend to favour political freedoms, thus eventually leading to democracy.

9 Here one should be aware of what all economists know and fear: a perfect free market economy must not be reached, for in it the rates of profit will be identical in all sectors, all resources will be used up, there will be no chance of innovation and equilibrium will be there in its static form.

10 The financial tycoon, as argued in Di Mario and Micocci (2015, and in preparation) can be likened, as Palma argues, to a rentier. In that sense, its presence is closer to how Adam Smith (1999, 2009) saw the class structure of his own time, and of capitalism.

11 See Samuels *et al.* (2014) and Di Mario and Micocci (2015, and in preparation).

12 Once again, Schumpeter had an intuition and a theory concerning the military, which we signal here without discussing it, for it would take us too far astray. See Schumpeter (1951).

13 Fortune had claimed it to have been the most discussed book of the year.

14 Sweezy claimed that managers could not gain such independence, and that fascism was capitalist. Yet we should carefully scrutinise the similarities with the USSR.

5 Managerialism

We mentioned earlier, in describing capitalism, Galbraith's 'technostructure'. Now we are going to see its modern and developed version in what we call from now a form of managerialism, and how it has gained economic, political and even cultural primacy. The definition of managerialism we give here is dependent, as is anything else, on the 'metaphysics of capitalism' in general (Micocci, 2009/2010, 2016), which should be clear by now. Thus, it does not depend on the title of one of the chapters (What is managerialism?) of Fleming's (2015) book, either.

Cunliffe (2009) has pointed out, recalling the philosopher Derrida (1978), that words derive their meaning from their opposite. In our case, neoliberalism characterises itself for rationality against irrationality; efficiency vs inefficiency; organisation against disorganisation. The crucial, psychological operation in the use of a term lies in the attitude of the majority of socialised human beings to privilege positive terms, which are wrongly considered true, in opposition to the opposite term, which is compelled to be false. The phenomenon of privileging one term – the positive one – means that the negative becomes a set of unquestioned norms, which favours one group over others. This is the case of managers who pretend to be associated with the term 'rational' as a positive and self-explanatory tool to enhance their interests and legitimise their role.

Cunliffe's argument leads us to the link between neoliberalism and managerialism. The explanation resides in the following paradox of a (il)legitimised power that is not legitimate, as portrayed by Drucker (1942, p. 64) in *The Future of Industrial Man*:

> In the modern corporation the decisive power, that of the managers, is derived from no one but the managers themselves controlled by nobody and nothing and responsible to no one. It is in the most literal sense unfounded, unjustified, uncontrolled and irresponsible power.

Managerialism in its popular sense started in the USA, where production and management techniques such as Taylorism, Fordism and Porter's theory were later extended worldwide. Technically speaking, management is the group of processes and tools implemented by managers to enhance a firm's performance in order to achieve higher profits. During the twentieth century, managers were considered as qualified/skilled administrators and their actions were interpreted as adequate, relevant and competent only within the limited area of firms, and only in this sense was their work seen as relevant to the economy.

According to Drucker (1973), a management boom emerged between the 1940s and the 1960s and changed society permanently because management became popular, legitimised and supported by institutional and social norms. This gave managers the right to hire and fire, give orders and exercise control over the workers in the interest of efficiency, productivity, profit or even for providing a service for the common good. With the rise of the shareholder system of ownership, which, as everybody knows, predates the twentieth century, the need to implement managerial techniques to increase the value of shares – that is, profit-oriented growth – helped the rise of 'predator' managers whose attitude towards the firms and far beyond changed (Goldstein, 2012). Indeed, this brought an enormous change in the theory of the firm itself, as testified by the works of Marris, Baumol and Williamson, and even Galbraith, whose thorough consideration is beside the point here. On the one hand, profitability prevaricated other performance dimensions of the firm, while, on the other, the introduction of the managerial role and techniques better exploited factors of production and labour forces by limiting their rights (including unionism, right of strikes, welfare, etc.). Such erosion of workers' and citizens' rights were conducted by conservative/paternalistic/lobbystic/ mainstream political forces influenced by managerialists.

Aglietta (2016) completes this brief overview of our contemporary times by succinctly considering present-day change, again especially in the Anglo-Saxon countries, which set the pace of the movement to come to other places. He confirms (p. 125) that the process of financialisation of the firm has had dramatic consequences in terms of corporate governance and human resource management practices. Yet, he adds a basic twist, which we have anticipated in Chapters 1–4: 'The managerial firm has been transformed into a finance-led firm.' The incentive proposed comes down to the maximisation of the market return of the company for shareholders (ibid.). The above is very important for us here for the given reason, even when we look at it together with what has been done to force common people and common people's capital to go into finance. This phenomenon has changed people's outlook on the firm as well as on society itself, and to the manager-entrepreneur, led by the popular misunderstanding of manager-entrepreneur-rich man that is so fundamental now. Aglietta (ibid.) notices that productivity is no longer boosted, as we have noted. The impact (p. 126) of financial liberalisation and deregulation has led to a fundamental shift in the governance of firms. All this, of course, in the popular mind needs a discussion of the present crises; we believe it, however, to be typical of capitalism in general, as repeatedly said, and we will pursue no such discussion.

Political and social factors brought managerialism to configure itself as a sort of ideology originated and used by managers to propose and eventually affirm their superiority in organising the factors of production, unquestionably imposing their practise onto all industries and to all fields of society; this is also labelled 'new managerialism'. According to Deetz, managerialism is 'a kind of systemic logic, a set of routine practices, and an ideology', which aims at enhancing efficiency through control (Deetz, 1992, p. 222). It is precisely this form of efficiency that is supposed to work at the economic, political, social and even personal level alike, which makes it most evidently akin to everything we have been discussing so far.

We should also bear in mind, yet again, that the current popular and media impression is that 'manager' coincides with 'entrepreneur' and is efficient, as fascists would say, and acts even more efficiently and impersonally than it used to. Thus, with the same logic described in Chapter 2 and onwards, you can, and indeed must, criticise predatory managers and entrepreneurs, but only replace them with better, milder and supposedly more human ones. Most importantly, however, most of the time they appear hard to criticise because they hold the position of inevitable interpreters of what comes down to be common wisdom (free enterprise and the like) in capitalism as we know it. (This is mythical language at its most popular and base.) They are the fascist dictators non-dictators, the '*vate*'[1] at work, and can be replaced only by another *vate*, for (fascist) natural inequality sees to it.

Klikauer (2015) argues that managerialism is generated by three components according to a formula as follows:

Management + Ideology + Expansion = Managerialism

Klikauer's formula represents two main components of managerialism: management (a fundamental component) and ideology (our present neoliberal component). A third component identified by Klikauer is expansion. We propose that this last should be replaced by a different one because 'expansion' is not an identifiable and stable characteristic in all contexts but can vary according to the consensus given to the sum of Management + Ideology. In addition, the formula seems to miss the resistance factor to the expansion of managerialism itself. For this reason, considering all we have said so far, we would rather propose the following formula:

(Management + Ideology) * Metaphysics = Managerialism

The metaphysics, being amenable to many occasions in the form of an ideological process, is the component of the formula that better portrays the manifestation of managerialism as a factor of expansion. Hoopes (2003) argues that managerialism has gone so far as to turn the US into a 'business civilisation'. The past national democratic political tradition, with its intellectual resources – Puritanism, republicanism, individualism, pragmatism – was emptied by the business power of corporations and their 'sophisticated social philosophy' that speaks the language of democracy. Whether or not the managers had spoken the language of 'democracy' or the politicians started to behave as managers with the further ability to make profit out of their political role, it is clear, as argued repeatedly, that managers and politicians started speaking the same (neoliberal) language.

The era of managerialism started with the affirmation of corporate managers in the management of the nation itself. The corporate approach to institutions reoriented their domestic and foreign policies. Take, for illustration purposes, the case of Charles Erwin Wilson, a General Motors' engineer, and his appointment to the seat of Secretary of Defense. As popularly known, during the recruitment interview he was asked to express his attitude towards an eventual 'conflict of interests' between the national interest and GM's interest. His answer became so emblematic that can be quoted from popular wisdom sources such as the internet: 'because for years I thought what was good for our country was good for General Motors, and vice versa' (Wikipedia, 2016). The statement of the coincidence of national and corporate interests ideally inaugurates neoliberalism in managerialism, and consequently a more coherent manifestation than before of their metaphysics in their communication.

Without mentioning the word 'neoliberalism', Hoopes (2003) attributes a 'holistic' *fil rouge* to the managerialism generated from the Harvard Business School of Dean Wallace Donhan down to the politics of George Bush (MBA at Harvard) and Mitt Romney. Hoopes (ibid.) portrays how managerial politicians inaugurated the era of the 'corporate politicians', in which managers sought to influence the institutional governance to affirm the corporate interests by enhancing the managerial knowledge owned by management. Managerial language had begun to be spoken by politicians and the media, automatically bringing a slandering attitude to the political institutions and persons that were traditional in the USA, and latent in Europe. Managerialist politicians express all this anew by freely using the neoliberal ideology beyond the corporate dimension. In other words, as we noticed more philosophically in Chapter 2, they seek to pervade society with the commodification of social relations. The unilateral imposition of their thinking and actions does not appear clearly because their ideas are homogeneous with the dominant intellectuality (Micocci, 2009/2010, 2016), which is poor enough for neoliberalism to appear as an ideology.

In fact, the metaphysics of managerialism shows itself, just as neoliberalism in general, in a particular use of language, which manifests itself, despite its appearance of professionalism, through an illogical and emptied terminology. Taptiklis (2005) proposes an interpretation of managerialism as intrinsically inimical to complexity because matrix structures burden professionals and its methods diminish human capability and potential. Management needs to operate, says Taptiklis, through three main artifices.

The first is the mystification of term, the misplacing the original meaning of words and/or the contradiction of the common rules in syntax – for example, in the mainstream conception of post-Fordist labour structure: the two poles are identified as security/flexibility, whereas they should be named security/insecurity or, alternatively, rigidity/flexibility. The way neoliberal language is used also misleads the status of workers.

The mystification of terms operated by managerialism serves neoliberalism by making democracy inconsistent, confusing the original conception of human values such as social participation, freedom and human dignity with mis-constructs, creating a negative culture towards independent thinking, free relationships and non-traded goods, which are banned and persecuted as Wrenn (2015) and Davies (2016) say in their own way:

> But the idea of bottom-up employee power also has a cultural function in democratic society at large, which explains why management ideologues greatly overstate it.

On the face of it, bottom-up power seems democratic and consistent with America's historic political culture. When employees bring their democratic values to work, managers assuage their feelings of lost freedom and dignity with the idea that the corporation is a bottom-up organisation, not the top-down hierarchy that in reality it is. A certain linguistic confusion in the management ideology helps accomplish this cultural function. Managerialism confuses 'power' in the physical sense of power to do the job with 'power' in the political sense of power over oneself and others. By emphasising the first sense of power, management gurus imply that employees also enjoy power in the latter sense.

Hoopes, 2003

The second artifice consists in the invention of terminology. Managerialism is very much engaged in terminology creation, paying specific attention to professions and technical activities. The introduction of new terms that characterise themselves as being unclear to the 'outsider' is a constant tactic. This is particularly true for the so-called 'new' or 'digital' economy, which continuously produces a number of new terms as part of its inane technical nature. With a growing amount of inconsistent terminology, managerialism promotes new professions, ways of saying things and contexts in which, as we all know, costs can be reduced within a general depression of workers' status and rights. The whole is not transparent because the terms used are not self-explanatory. In a global market (again, as usual with neoliberalism, this is pretended or presumed and rarely proved), managerialism tends to obscure communication while pretending to increase credibility and produce a better image of the corporate/institutional entity. The continuously enlarged terminology is manifest in technical documentation, which tends to homogenise the world by the use of English language, which is a salient part of its assumption to be part of a global market.[2] The homogenised terminology of managerialism can make a big contribution in limiting who is excluded from managerial fields, thus excluding all those that cannot have access to the newest linguistic invention of terms.

The third artifice is the monopoly of formal and informal means of communication. The terminology, language and lexicons of managerialism are created and supported by a plethora of mainstream ideologists, professionals and, sometimes, intellectuals who are responsible for the monopoly of such formal and informal means of communications. Peters (2001, p. 119), for instance, considers this dimension of neoliberalism as a 'project of postmodernity' that is characterised by 'the master narrative to legitimate an extreme form of economic rationalism'.

Poole (2006) described this process addressing one of the most inflated terms of common parlance and, naturally, of managerialism – 'human resources' – just to explain things by means of a relevant example:

> the template of 'natural resources' must, further, be to blame for the modern barbarism of the corporate term 'human resources'. To call human beings 'resources', firstly, is to deny their existence as individuals, since any one person will not spring up again once worn out; people are 'resources' only insofar as they are thought of as a breeding population, like rabbits or chickens. 'Human resources', first recorded in 1961, eventually succeeded the term 'manpower' in business parlance; the effect was merely to replace a crude sexism with a more generalised rhetorical violence. People considered as 'human resources' are mere instruments of a higher will. Compare the Nazi vocabulary of 'human material' [men – schenmaterial] and 'liquidation' [liquidieren], recasting murder as the realisation of profit; if 'natural resources' evinces merely as blithe disregard for the environment, 'human resources' contains an echo of totalitarian Unspeak.[3]

> Ibid., p. 66

Alvesson and Spicer (2016) address the diffuse '*if not, a dominant*' (p. 17, emphasis added) compliance of academics to managerialism. They consider it to be 'a mystery' because it is unexpected that a high-status group with a strong work commitment shows such a non-critical acceptance of change. (See also the Appendix, this volume.) They argue that:

> the (un)conditional surrender of professional autonomy can be explained by looking at the role which power plays. Clearly exercises of coercive power in the form of increasing managerial hierarchy, the use of incentives such as bonuses for publication and increasingly punitive punishments for 'non-performance' have been important. But this would not have worked if it was not backed up by a particular conception of research rising rapidly to the top of the agenda of both formal and informal discussions in universities. This has been further underpinned by a defeatist acceptance of neoliberal ideas, which are then combined with other 'traditional' academic values such as competition, excellence as well as a wider desire for grandiosity. All this is made personal – as research work has morphed into identity work. It has been further reinforced by new technologies which can immediately make one's research performance visible.
>
> Ibid., pp. 16–17

By revealing the link between managerialism and neoliberalism in academia, Alvesson and Spicer conclude that 'it has created a glut of research which is uninteresting and says little of significance to a larger audience' and add 'What this suggests is that if we are indeed serious about creating scholarship which is both more interesting and more engaging, then simply demanding academics start being interesting and engaging is unlikely to work' (ibid., p. 42).

The above contribution improves upon another work of Alvesson (2013), which we can use here for brevity purposes. *The Triumph of Emptiness* addresses the need for rethinking some of the basic concepts of Western societies in our time, for instance, liberalism, democracy, political economy and, last but not least, equality.

But I think that most people should be concerned with more than just landing and keeping a job or experiencing acceptance and membership in academia; and thus having something to say should be vital.

By 'say' I mean that there are knowledge contributions that an audience of people outside a specialized academic setting would be inclined to read and find interesting and relevant for their organizational life. This does not necessarily mean managers, but could be professionals, union representatives or general members of the public with some intellectual interest.

Alvesson, 2012, p. 79; Harris, 2014

The 'linguistic confusion' created by managerialism functions to free such academicians from objective judgement and allows them to perpetrate it despite failing results in practice. The mystification of terminology operated in the theory is crucial to drive attention away from the reality of neoliberal fallacy. In practice, managers are exonerated from their responsibility at different levels (see also Black, 2014). Proponents of managerialism such as *Harvard Business Review*'s former editor Magretta (2012, p. 3), claim that 'We all learn to think like managers, even if that's not what we're called.'

In managerial regimes, managerialism justifies its predominance on the grounds of managing a group's superior education and exclusive possession of 'people in positions of institutional power' (ibid., p. 4). Managerialists pretend to have an advanced knowledge and the know-how deemed necessary to the efficient running of organisations. The rise of senior managers and their 'neoliberal institutionalisation' helps them occupy a peculiar space in firms: they sit in a higher place than traditional management, ownership and workforce. Such space is also becoming increasingly relevant in public life.

According to others of its critics (Locke, 2011; Locke and Spender, 2011), managerialism is an expression of a special group – management – that secures itself ruthlessly and systemically in an organisation. As an effect, owners are deprived of decision-making power (Goldstein, 2012) and workers of their ability to resist managerial brutality and control (Braverman, 1974; Locke, 2011). Radical scholarship sees the rise of managerialism as a response to people's resistance in society and, more specifically, workers' opposition against managerial regimes (Chomsky, 1967; Karlsson, 2012). 'During Herbert Hoover's years as Secretary of Commerce and then as president, managerialism was further honed, until it became the sword's-point of reform in the Roosevelt era. Managerialism was credited with the prosperity of the Eisenhower 1950s' (Scott and Hart, 1991, p. 40).

In such a general environment, and given the new roles taken and everything we have been saying so far, it was inevitable that managers had to intervene in politics to grant efficiency. Indeed, their presence becomes utterly necessary if we all agree on the goals, the programmes are smoky enough and the system lacks efficiency. This is precisely what neoliberalism is all about, if what has been argued in the preceding pages is correct. It is also identical with fascism in this respect.

The post-fascist-era rise of the managers' ideological interests in politics coincides then with the need to establish a neoliberal world order governed by international financial institutions, with a monopoly of communication and the deregulation of labour policies added. We have seen the origin of all this. The presence of managers in the political institutions and in public companies has a circular, crucial role in the motivations towards the privatisation of public and non-profit entities and also in the management of vital community-based resources such as water, energy, food production and patents.

The pervading characteristic of managerialism, in sum, is the proven capability of managers to make permeable what before them was not permeable, negotiable and tradable: public goods, welfare, water, housing, health care and all sorts of human rights. The pervasiveness of this view, and the imposition of managerialism adopted by individuals, delineate even more than what we have called a *vate*. We are discussing a manager more as a 'dux', a leader, the man in command with many sherpas (another fashionable word) whose brains are mere tools to achieve the purpose at hand. This has transformed managers into a 'management caste' in society (Locke and Spender, 2011). Democracy, in such a (fascist) natural inequality, need not be applied or sought. All you need is to achieve, exerting feasibility and rationality (efficiency).

The choice of the word 'dux' is not casual.[4] The term has undergone several political usages and interpretations through the ages to reach a new modern notoriety with the Italian fascist dictator Mussolini, who used the title of *dux* (*duce* in Italian) to represent his leadership. The concept itself, as with its practise, is neither new nor unused in capitalism; on the contrary, as explained in the preceding pages. By dux we also mean, naturally, the fascist interpreter or *vate*, the democratic/non-democratic leader of present-day oligarchies and parties all over Europe and beyond, so well explained by Gentile (1996). In other words, 'Leadership might be a form of damaged and ideological recognition, but it remains – perhaps precisely because of this quality – vital for management and managerialism' (Locke and Spender, 2011; Klikauer, 2013).

It is no surprise, as a consequence, that management sees this as something that informs reality. According to managerial doctrine, in order to manage, management 'does not need good theory' because it is management itself that 'gives you today's marching orders' (Magretta, 2012: 10). In a true 'military-equals-management' style, management gives marching orders and all followers have to do is to follow 'The Great Leader' (e.g. Kolditz, 2009; Gutstein, 2009). That is what managers are for, after all.

The openly fascist-like practices of managerialism manifest mainly in an 'oppressive climate' that is the hinge between the theory of human resources and the practise of the dynamics between capital and labour. Taptiklis (2005) gives the example of McKinsey & Company as a mainstream entity that has remained central throughout the last 50 years of managerialism's ascendency, together with its journal, the *McKinsey Quarterly*. He focuses on an article by Bryan and Joyce (2005) entitled 'Big

Corporations Must Make Sweeping Organisational Changes to Get the Best from Their Professionals', published as a critique to managerialism that emanates from a leading mainstream journal.

The analysis of Taptiklis (2005) on the 'nature of managerialism' identifies the main features that managerialism adopts towards people in organisation and society. This only reinforces, confirms and restates what we have been saying so far. We mention the following for the sake of completeness:

1 *lofty superiority*. There is no trace of humility. Managerialism knows what is best for people in organisations, and admits of no criticism or self-doubt. It positions itself in a sphere above and beyond normal human existence;

2 *disdain for ordinary human intercourse*. Managerialism has no time for the complexities, subtleties and uncertainties of human behaviour or of human relationships. Any communication that is not planned or formalised is a waste of time and must be eliminated. Social networks between professionals that formed spontaneously should be abandoned in favour of formal relationships;

3 *blind optimism about the future*, coupled with the possibility of interpreting the present through the past – through memory, history, habit, recognition of failure or reflection – is simply ignored. Managerialists are blindly optimistic: whatever happened before has no possible bearing on what can be made to happen now;

4 *belief that productive human behaviours are always monetised*. Discussing the exchange of knowledge, Bryan and Joyce ask, 'What's the best way of encouraging strangers to exchange valuable things?' (Bryan and Joyce, 2005, p. 30). In their world, the answer could not be community responsibility. It is, 'of course, markets [!]. The trick is to take the market inside the company' (ibid., exclamation mark added). (The word 'trick' perhaps acknowledges that only supernatural wizardry could ever make it happen);

5   *anti-humanity*. Finally, the most striking characteristic of managerialism is its anti-humanity. The only human behaviours that are recognised are those that serve the mechanical needs of the organisation. There is no room for doubt; for pain; for hesitation; for determination; for denial; for acceptance; for discovery; 'it then develops models and prescribes solutions only in terms of its own artifice' (ibid., pp. 4–5).

This, to our metaphysics of capitalism, is simply the application of the metaphysics itself. However, the fact that it can be pronounced anti-human makes it thoroughly fascinating to the fake courage nurtured by fascism (and, of course, managerialism). Plus, it looks feasible and rational, and its achievement looks like a victory. The openly fascist character of managerialism expresses its most evident effects in the area of industrial relations, where managerialism originated as management and expanded through pre-capitalist institutions and fascist practices (Micocci 2009/2010; Preston, 2001). It can best be summarised with one of the most well-known slogans created by Mussolini: *Credere, obbedire, combattere* [Believe, obey and concentrate on the struggle]. Similar claims were made of Hitler's *Mein Kampf* [*My Battle*], which uses the same fascist mythical language. The Nazis and their engagement in developing an efficient, and at the same time illogical and un-human, industrial society, was meant to respond to the 'commonsensical' requisites of productivity, profitability and harmony. Such Nazi claims allowed the illogic and nonsensical atrocities of the times of Hitler, as well as of those the present day. In this direction, Drucker (1942, pp. 107–8) argues that:

> Unless we realise that the essence of Nazism is also an attempt to solve a universal problem of Western civilisation – that of the industrial society – and that the basic principles on which the Nazis base this attempt are also in no way confined to Germany, we do not know what we fight for or what we fight against ... The war is being fought for the structure of industrial society – its basic principles, its purposes, and its institutions.

Joseph (2010: 679) analyses the exemplary case of the pilots' strike in Indian private airlines in September 2009 to establish empirically the reality of the existence of what he calls 'strategic *militant* managerialism'. The union mobilisation process is examined looking at the market-driven recession in the aviation context. The fact stressed in the analysis is the action of dismissal of two pilot leaders decided by the management in the midst of a union mobilisation. This, to Joseph, can be termed as: '*militant* managerialism' because it operates to achieve a 'regulated orderliness normative frame' (emphasis original). Joseph (ibid.) explains that 'managerialism, in its *militant* version, aims at establishing order, stability and control which implies to ignore the conflict rather than to understand the reasons of conflict'. Militant managerialism implements a mode of functioning of industrial relations we can call 'the *Hard Positional Bargaining mode*' (see Joseph, 2010: 679, emphasis original, and Fisher *et al.*, 1987), where disputants are perceived as adversaries and labelled 'labour terrorists'; the goal is the victory over workers' representation because the union should be eliminated: even if the firm has to be closed down'. To get there, militant managerialism pursues a 'divide and rule' strategy ('expat pilots versus indigenous pilots, absenting pilots versus on duty pilots, pilots versus other airline staff, management versus pilots, customers versus pilots, state agencies versus agitating pilots') (Joseph, 2010: 679).

> *Militant* managerialism engages in various forms of gamesmanship and brinkmanship (dismissal of key union leaders), denigrates adversaries (denounce and decry agitating pilots in the media, states sudden stoppages are anti customer and advantageous to competitors), takes vindictive action (dismissal of more pilots). *Militant* managerialism sees unions as subversive and pilots as dispensable commodities. The language of *militant* managerialism used to challenge the pilot action is also strong and provocative sabotage, illegal act, blackmail, labour terrorists, threat of more sackings, closure, condemnation of inconvenience to travelling public. The 'demonization' of pilot leaders and agitationists using

terrorist imagery amplified by similar sentiments expressed by executives and leaders of other airlines through the electronic and print media served to evoke strong negative reactions towards not only union mobilization efforts but also the disruptive protest action of mass absence on sick leave demanding the reinstatement of dismissed pilot leaders.

Ibid., emphasis original

This ruthless attitude to conflict is easily referred to and explained by the vulgar Hegelian character of the metaphysics of capitalism. The preservation of the term 'other' without its content (for it means diversity in capitalist economic and general reality) allows those in power to transform any form of conflict: dialectical mediations (all we have in capitalism) are changed into apparent and untrue catastrophic ruptures with disappearance, which require the use of the extreme end of the range of mediation means available. That is also how wars are justified: bombing and invading appear as the only means by which 'they' can be brought to an agreement, a mediation. A most telling case is that of the pathetic defeat of the Tsipras Cabinet by the EU authorities, which teaches us that, paradoxically, reasonableness and moderation can do nothing to stop the efficient logic of managerialism and its false catastrophes always impending. The compromise is always at one extreme of the range of solutions available: that held by those in power.

When brutality is not used, managerialism adopts a concessionary system of economic and social relations where there are no permanent rights, but a 'case by case' authorisation of workers by managers. The Fordist organisation of work is made of consent and control (Braverman, 1974) but also of pre-capitalist institutions relations – a typical feature of the metaphysics of capitalism (Micocci, 2009/2010, 2016) where human relations are configured with contours of king/servants and regulator vs the spy and enemy. This latter manifests itself in the concessionary system where 'case by case' authorisation of managers is needed for workers to act outside the production line.

The concessionary system reminds us, in fact, of the '*octroyée*' constitutional order, which is known for falsely being a constitutional order because rights for all are not granted unless given by the 'goodwill' of the monarch. This system of rights of managerialism is crucial to establish the role of the dux, the man in command from whom all spheres of human activities depend. The false complexity of both institutional and economic organisations that is embodied in the increasing number of professional positions, departments and sections is proportional to their irrelevancy given the factual maximum authority of the CEO, a 'postmodern dux' who governs according to the strict values of managerialism. According to Forst (2010), there are forms of 'concessionary' system characterised by both liberating/repressive aims because 'toleration appears to be a strategic, or at least a hierarchical policy designed to prevent general and equal rights, but to give specific permissions that are granted, and that can always be revoked' (pp. 220ff).

A further main component of the metaphysics of capitalism we wish to underline here is the introduction of the so-called imaginative communication within the corporate world – in particular, the emptiest of them all, the 'vision'. Vision statements can be defined as the 'corporate manifesto' that has replaced the social manifestos in the communication of workers because it is intended to be imposed universally, and the same 'imposition' or 'concessionary' communication is meant to be used for institutions and social entities as well.

Grey (1999) highlights the oppressive character of managerialism's project. Managerialism's false universalisation not only is oppressive, it also seeks to eliminate the class character of managerial capitalism. Recently, some media noise was provoked by an academic speech given by the CEO of the National Electrical Company in Italy, which can be taken as a neat example of how managerialism in theory and practice materialises in present-day neoliberal institutions: the national institutions. The government, as said in theory earlier, decided the appointment of such a 'manager'. The rising role of this person incarnates the ideal corporate career figure and development and the 'academic institutions' legitimate managerialism, giving it a space and identifying this managerial individual as an example in/for academia.

For a better understanding of Starace's speech to the students of LUISS Business School on 14 April, we report his words:

> Per cambiare un'organizzazione ci vuole un gruppo sufficiente di persone convinte di questo cambiamento, non è necessario sia la maggioranza, basta un manipolo di cambiatori. Poi vanno individuati i gangli di controllo dell'organizzazione che si vuole cambiare e bisogna distruggere fisicamente questi centri di potere. Per farlo, ci vogliono i cambiatori che vanno infilati lì dentro, dando ad essi una visibilità sproporzionata rispetto al loro status aziendale, creando quindi malessere all'interno dell'organizzazione dei gangli che si vuole distruggere. Appena questo malessere diventa sufficientemente manifesto, si colpiscono le persone opposte al cambiamento, e la cosa va fatta nella maniera più plateale e manifesta possibile, sicché da ispirare paura o esempi positivi nel resto dell'organizzazione. Questa cosa va fatta in fretta, con decisione e senza nessuna requie, e dopo pochi mesi l'organizzazione capisce perché alla gente non piace soffrire. Quando capiscono che la strada è un'altra, tutto sommato si convincono miracolosamente e vanno tutti lì. È facile. [Applausi].
>
> [Transl.: In order to change an organisation it is necessary a sufficient group of persons are convinced of such change. They must not necessarily constitute the majority, all we need is a bunch of change-minded people. Then the centres of control of the organisation we want to change must be individuated, for they must be physically destroyed. To do so, we need the changers to be inserted inside there, and we must give them a visibility that is disproportionate to their power within the firm, thus creating malaise within the power centres we want to destroy. As soon as such malaise gets sufficiently evident, we dismiss the people who oppose the change, which must be done in the most theatrical and

evident way we can, in order to instil fear or positive examples in the organisation. Such a thing must be done as quickly as possible, with decision and giving no rest, and after a few months the organisation understands, because people do not like to suffer. When they realise that the path to follow is changed, they miraculously convince themselves and they all go the right direction. It is easy. (Ovation)]

It is worth our while pointing out that the words Starace uses are the typical words of fascist documents and of Mussolini's propaganda journalism, and so are the strategies he suggests. They also correspond to the words and strategies of Italian *Neo-fascismo*, which even invented a political line, a '*strategia della tensione*' [a strategy of tension-making] that led to the terrorist massacres of the 1970s in Italy. A study of this aspect, which cannot be done here, would be a worthwhile undertaking.

In Italy, when a neoliberal regime replaced Silvio Berlusconi's government with Monti's neoliberal technocracy (Di Mario, 2015), the majority of the press kept serving the same corporate interests in a subordinate way. Thus it should not come as a surprise that Starace's speech has been largely ignored by the Italian media, general public and, above all, by academic institutions. LUISS University, first of all, did not make any excuse for his bad teaching. Yet, the news did not pass unobserved in Chile, where the newspaper *El Mostrador Mercados*, on 20 May 2016, explained Starace's speech and titled the piece 'The fascist recipe of Starace for doing business'.

In Italy, the appointment of Starace by the Democratic Party Secretary and (at the time) Premier Matteo Renzi shows us that a symbolic point of perfect matching has been reached between the fascist heritage and the 'material' practice of managerialism in the neoliberal trajectory. The fascist heritage and genre is also put into sharp relief, ironically, by the fact that Francesco Starace, the press alleged,[5] might even have family ties with Achille Starace (at least he bears an identical family name), the fascist hierarch and ideological leader. Achille Starace was not an ordinary hierarch. Among other things, he helped conduct the war against Ethiopia. It does not come as a surprise that less than a century later someone like him, bearing the same name, CEO of the National Electrical and Energy company, can use similar words in a different context.

Notes

1 This is an Italian word referring to he/she whom sees what is there but we common mortals do not see. It became popular during World War I and with the poet D'Annunzio.
2 See, yet again, Moretti and Pestre (2015) for a most important, exemplary and blatant case.
3 Nassau Senior (1838) spoke of a 'mental capital', and must likely be credited as at least one of the inventors of these absurdities, which the metaphysics of capitalism has multiplied and made to look innocent. We also pointed the reader earlier to their Stalinist pedigree.
4 From the Latin *duco*, lead.
5 We performed no accurate check of this, for it is irrelevant and exemplary only, i.e. secondary.

6 Conclusions

There is an evident continuity through all the phases of capitalism that calls for a deeper explanation than the current mainstream, and mainstream Marxist banality, of the production and exchange of commodities. What is happening at present in the logic of capital valorisation is precisely the decline of commodity production – at least in the developed West. The complex set of phenomena we refer to as financialisation has gained the upper hand, and governments are desperate to convince the remaining capitalists who deal in material production to stay in business – that is, to forgo the high rates of capital multiplication that finance grants in order to keep producing commodities domestically for a much lower rate of profit. Hence the importance, to help them keep on, of reducing labour rights and of a self-secure attitude such as the one embodied in neoliberalism. In this task, governments can count on most media, although the assessment of their effectiveness is close to the impossible (see Grossi, 2011).

Not only do finance and capital represent the most independently metaphysical items of present-day capitalism (see Micocci, 2009/2010, 2011a, 2011b, 2012, 2016, and from a different, but always anti-Hegelian perspective, Rosenthal, 1998), but also the very absurd, and unthinkable to a sound mind, issue of governments having to defend material production (nobody, in fact, however rich, can live without material products, most of which, with our present technology, few of us can produce independently) represents the stupid questions the metaphysics of capitalism corners itself into, and shows the sad gullibility of those who discuss them. Surely, as long as under-developed nations or extremely poor working masses exist, the problem appears solvable by means of political expansion. Banking on that, however, would be very imprudent. People in power and their lackeys can only, therefore, stick to the neolib-eral policies that increase inequalities while increasing the grip of the state over the economy and politics. All governments seek to do that, whatever their political stand.

We are not interested, in these pages, in the actual solutions that might be adopted to solve this practical set of problems, however. Our purpose here has been solely to notice, search and point out that the whole historical nature and actual development of capitalism shows a common character. Such character, in the typical, dismaying intellectual poverty and lack of fantasy of capitalism as we know it, can be reduced to the set of common phenomena we call the general metaphysics of capitalism. In this capitalism,[1] societies and states are viewed as organic communi-ties striving for efficiency, corporatism is sought, practised or proposed (this is often smuggled in as the importance of social peace – efficiency again – for the sake, for instance, of the macroeconomic fundamentals); ethics is invoked all the time and, as if that were not silly enough at the political level, the evident monstrosity of business ethics is also invoked; inter-national relations are operated with the aim to reach a solution that appears as a mediation, and therefore wars are continuously made against those who do not comply, especially of the strong against the weak; non-state forms of human organisation are written off as unthinkable, while at the same time pockets of difference are pushed towards a form that is then erased by exter-mination (mercifully renamed humanitarian war, or anti-terrorism special laws and actions); the 'other' – commonly named the 'diverse', because, as repeatedly said, capitalism knows of no difference between these two fundamental terms in politics – is seen, as a consequence, either as a threat or as an ally.

All the above are possible because metaphysical concepts replace sound ideas as well as material items. The metaphysics of capitalism, while pushing its economic form towards the highest degree of efficiency in the valorisation of capital (most evidently and fashionably represented currently, as said repeatedly, by the so-called financialisation), produces an endless array of what Cassirer (1962) more narrowly but efficaciously called items of mythical language: we can intellectually identify them with the vulgar Hegelianism of all capitalist manifestations. Only thus can all the absurdities listed above gain credibility, and appear as the bread and butter of capitalist political and economic doings. All this is typical of the fascist understanding of capitalism, if we conceptualise capitalism, as we have sought to do in the present volume, as a logically flawed metaphysics, and fascism as capitalism's most obvious form, since this last lost its capacity to think radically.

An alternative, in theory – and therefore in practice if, as we submit here, capitalism is based on a, however flawed, intellectuality – would have been possible, basing all efforts upon the Enlightenment's libertarian, sceptical and Epicurean streaks of thought and, above all, upon the work of Karl Marx (see Micocci, 2016). But Marx has been hijacked by a strict Hegelian reading that, however implausible and politically impotent, is perfectly consonant with the dominant intellectuality of capitalism, its metaphysics. With Marx, Enlightenment thinkers have been also relegated to an erudite corner. Among the reasons that might have determined such a sad occurrence, we wish to point out to the reader here the sacred fear that Marxists have of the anarchist consequences of Marx's own words. One can easily see how perfectly coherent this is with the capitalist (fascist) horror of non-state human groupings, of revolution as a Kantian real opposition that erases the past and, of course, of individual emancipation.[2]

Thus capitalism has been falsely sterilised from fascism. Capitalism as we know it has misunderstood this last term by means of a typically capitalist convoluted metonymy: racism, wars of aggression and expansion, mass organisation of the population, dictatorship have become its qualifying features, and a way to exorcise it as well as to attack all sorts of cruel dictatorships by brandishing the spectre of this term. Such misunderstanding comes down to a way to imagine a reality that is perfectly analogous in its intellectual structures to the way capitalism imagines reality in general (Micocci, 2009/2010, 2016). As a consequence, it is also a way to force one to believe, or not to waste time doubting, the fascist idea that societies are organic and historically justified (today, the word 'community' is used and abused to that purpose), and that states[3] compete with each other in the international arena, seeking to keep their heads from sinking and drowning by a mixture of collaboration and conflict that eerily alludes to Schmitt's own conception.

There would be no need to even discuss, of course, the fact that the economies of all countries, however effectual their free market propaganda, are managed, monopolies (the fascist plutocracy) are (formally) abhorred, banks are kept under control and/or protected even when one of them, as, for instance, Northern Rock, is occasionally left to sink as a warning to all. Consumption is refined by educating the masses, even by giving the opposition a chance to play a leading role, as for safe, or ethical, or ecological food or banking. This is so perfectly coherent with the fascist organic conception of society that it needs no further discussion.

Populations are grouped under the 'civilisation' label, the origins of which are in the fascist myths and the relative mythical language, of which Huntington's 'clash of civilisation' has been only a recent, famously disgusting instance. Even the empty Marxist rhetoric of class struggle (which is, and only can be, revolutionarily empty as long as it is conceived in a dialectical way; see Micocci, 2009/2010, 2012, 2016) has been substituted by the fascist empty rhetoric of class peace as a community reaction to the terrible challenges ahead (corporatism with fascist rhetoric), while new items have been added to the new, wider conception of corporation, with their inevitable results in terms of increasing inequality, as Benn Michaels (2008) well summarises.

All this is, as pointed out several times, presided over by the preponderance of finance. This last not only offers an avenue for dazzlingly high rates of multiplication of capital's value, displacing material production and offering neoliberalism's reactionary side a chance to operate. The preponderance of finance has also allowed the metaphysics of capitalism to be epitomised in a language that looks very much like Cassirer's mythical language and Merker's vulgar Hegelian absurdities. The more wrong and the more imprecise it gets, the better it strikes the perverted chords of the flawed collective mentality of capitalism. Let us say it in a plain way: to us, the main problem of the metaphysics of capitalism is that it produces an anti-individual mentality, a collective (limited) set of feelings and a collective (limited) language, which can be iterated for ever.

As a result, capitalism as we know it looks like a mixture of the warning put forward by Marcuse (1967), Debord (2004) and Reich (1970), who have been discussed at length in the past and never seriously pondered and acted upon by Westerners. That is because capitalism's typical incapacity to see, and describe, radical concepts (Micocci, 2016) makes it impotent to put things in the simple, radical way with which they present themselves in nature. The result is that we get the intellectuals to talk, instead of reality in general, of the single problems of neoliberal times, and how they can be solved without subversive consequences. The outcome of this typically capitalist move is not only the self-serving simplification of reality by over-complication. It also lends an intellectual dignity and credibility to neoliberalism, which can now drag in its intellectual emptiness the masses of those who are in its favour as well as the masses of those who are against it. Both factions are compelled to stick to neoliberalism's language and to its structures of thought, thus replicating the iterative pattern of the metaphysics of capitalism. Yet, there is an armed force to secure the (un)validity of the neoliberal metaphysical language, which is embodied by the managerialists.

The contemporary dominance of managerialism manifests itself in the economic, political and cultural sectors with its pervading, uncontrolled (Drucker, 1942) and unpredictable mode. Managerialism is clearly a manifestation of the metaphysics of capitalism because it relies on neoliberal ideology to deprive all things and all reasoning of their ontological connection to reality (Micocci, 2008, 2010, 2016). Being practical, managerialism uses pragmatism to set off ontology and elaborate economic theories and its derivative disciplines such as strategic management, human resource management, organisational behaviour, just to mention a few.

Such theories and practices use a terminology that privileges neoliberal terms (rationality, efficiency, organisation) in opposition to other neologies (irrationality, inefficiency, disorganisation); then they make a privileged choice for their own (self-explanatory) terminology, turn this dichotomy into opposition (Cunliffe, 2009) and, finally, establish an authoritarian set of values and governance in the name of industrial production. From a traditionalist Marxist perspective, this is the old conflict between capital and labour, which has partially been dismantled by some Marxist and neo-Marxist scholarship including political economists and scientists, sociologists, philosophers and others. These latter have rather participated in reorienting the interests of 'conformist'[4] academicians (Alvesson and Spicer, 2016) in what we can sum up as some Master of Business Administration (MBA) disciplines and their self-appointed pretence of being 'the science' – or the doctrine.

The combination of entrepreneurial intents and company goals within a metaphysical intellectual framework links managerialism, fascism and, naturally, neoliberalism. Managerialism is the result of the combination of management and ideology, which needs a multiplier of metaphysics to manifest. As with neoliberalism in general, the unilateral dominant intellectuality (*pensee unique*) of the metaphysics of capitalism uses of a language made up of artifices and methods to diminish human capability and its potential to emancipate humanity. The 'management caste' in society (Locke and Spender, 2011) does not need democracy, just as the neoliberal technocracy (Di Mario, 2015). It self-legitimises itself by applying feasibility and rationality (efficiency), but requires a dux to act in a 'military-equals-management' style. The ruthless attitude to conflict of managerialism and its oppressive character (Grey, 1999) can equally apply to a nation-state, private airlines or a national electrical company. The silence of neoliberal journalism and media does not come as a surprise. It is just another instance of *pensiero unico/pensee unique*.

All that we have succinctly endeavoured to describe here looks to us to be equivalent to fascism. This last we propose as a working hypothesis that needs to be studied thoroughly, which the present text cannot, obviously, do. The truly important question, however, is that even if capitalism and present-day neoliberal capitalism were not fascist, yet they look terrifying, just as they always did. What worries us is not the horrifying nature of its single characteristics: rather, we are petrified by the fact that those who claim to be in opposition to it partake of the same mental structure as those who defend it. It appears doomsday may be upon us.

As if matters were not bad enough, there is a further supreme irony. The world is becoming repopulated by all sorts of fascist and Nazist parties and grassroots organisations. They become bolder in their claims and in their actions by the day; they are in the open in many countries and have even assumed power. They, however, if everything we have been proposing here is true, are fighting for what they already have. Their struggles, and the sufferings that are entailed, only have a symbolic value: to give the name to the thing, it is capitalism as we know it.

Notes

1 Which likely is not what Adam Smith, Karl Marx and John Stuart Mill envisaged, we suggest.
2 Just to remind the reader: the individualistic approach of mainstream economics is, in fact, its opposite, for it is based on the assumption that the human mass we find in the market is homogeneous. Each person is an arithmetical nth of the whole.
3 This is perfectly compatible with nationalism: nation-states can be made, unmade and reinvented at leisure, and new conflicts argued about by splitting the ethnical or independentist hair.
4 This category includes the orthodox, conservative and mainstream scholars of the right and left.

Appendix
A telling episode

Understanding fascism in terms of the metaphysics of capitalism, and even in terms of Cassirer's narrower mythical language, might prove a difficult exercise to people from non-fascist, non-Latin or non-Catholic backgrounds. Yet the Catholic condition that plagues most fascisms does not justify in any way the superficial observation some might put forward that fascism is a typically Catholic cultural phenomenon that does not apply to capitalism in general. Our contention, it is worth repeating, is that the metaphysics of capitalism replicates in a more general – and, indeed, in an all-encompassing way – the flawed processes of the fascist ideas and actual policies because both have capitalism as we know it and its stunted intellectuality as their origin. The issues at stake in the following story should be easily recognised by all types of people.

A truly relevant difficulty, which concerns everybody from any cultural background, comes from the fact that the metaphysics is the same thing as capitalism in general (see Micocci, 2016), which makes it hard to pin it down for the non-independent eye – that is, the eye used to the dominant routine. The fascist argument, with its devious and multiform appearance, is a further complication. Hopefully, to help understand the general discourse, we briefly outline here the kind of intellectual environment that nurtured fascism by offering the following, Italian, edifying episode. The instructive part lies in its banality, which is precisely what we want to show here. It is through banality that fascism and neoliberalism win the day.

In other words, actual historical fascisms are special cases of a generalised intellectual mode that took, and takes even now, numerous cultural forms in the various countries that have developed, or want to do so, capitalistically. We should never forget that capitalism has been able to move from Protestant, to Catholic, to Orthodox countries, to finally land in Muslim environments[1] and in the People's Republic of China, whatever dominant culture and ideology are at present.

The episode below is telling (but remains an episode with no ambition to mean any more than an exemplary illustration) because it not only involves cultural aspects and persons formally and institutionally recognised as intellectually and culturally above average, but also illustrates the very creation, use and habituation to the many and varied nationalistic myths the various forms of capitalism throw out. The outcomes differ in formal terms, but all come down to the creation of a common ancestry (some might like to see it as akin to Anderson's imagined communities), the main characteristic of which, despite cultural diversities, is the consonance to the metaphysics of capitalism. The reader should therefore seek to place what we are about to tell here within the more general, theoretical framework sketched in the body of the volume.

In summer 2015 the present authors were at the European Society for the History of Economic Thought (ESHET) conference in Rome. At a presentation one afternoon, they listened to a long mention of Alessandro Manzoni (1785–1873), the canonical nineteenth-century Italian writer. Without consulting each other, the two authors raised their hands independently and intervened to object to the distorting use of Italian literature entailed by acknowledging Manzoni as a good writer. Manzoni was, in fact, a Catholic mediocre, whimpering, meaningless and, above all, boring committer of ink to paper transformed by all the various Italian states into a symbol of Italianness and expositor of the Italian culture and language. This they did by involving him into the political issue of making up the Italian language, first,[2] and, second, by the compulsory reading in all types and levels of schools, to this day, of his unbearable novel *I Promessi Sposi*

(*The Betrothed*).[3] His fame has obscured – that being the true intent of all Italian regimes – not only capable writers, but above all writers who were meaningful and radical (just think of Giacomo Leopardi or Federico De Roberto).

The presenters defended themselves from our attacks in the debate, but after the end of that official session a bunch of Italians gathered around the present authors to informally admit that they were not that wrong after all. Pity they did that after all foreigners had left, and in Italian (i.e. stealthily, just in case some could witness), in cowardly fashion. They stealthily did something else, too, as the reader will shortly discover. The funny and sad aspect of this part of the story is that the whole thing mattered very little because Manzoni (especially and deservedly his *Betrothed*) is very little known outside Italy, and no foreigner could grasp the true importance of the discussion.

The next day of the conference the present authors were at lunch with an American friend. In English, they were relating the episode, adding to it the negative impact on Italian history of the Catholic Church. A well-known professor of economics from Italy came sitting at the otherwise empty table, but at a one chair distance. She pretended not to be interested in the conversation, but at a certain point she could no longer help it and exploded. In Italian, she turned to Andrea Micocci uttering one of the most easily translatable expressions of the capitalist elementarised set of logical tools: '*Se non-ti piace, perché non-te ne vai?*' ['If you don't like it, why don't you go?']. The present authors were, needless to say, not intimidated, and the episode was drawn to a close. Never offend Manzoni or the Catholic Church for too long is the message.

If the lady had not been in a fury, or pursuing a sense of duty too high to mind elementary politeness, she would not have intruded in a conversation that was not hers, and she would have done it anyway in the language of that conversation – English – apologising first. Second, she had come to our table despite most other tables being free. One is led to hypothesise that she meant to come to scold us. If so, she must have been directed by the protagonists of the episode of the day before, at which she had not been present. The subject was, evidently, too important to let it pass unnoticed. It needed the intervention of a full professor.

The story gives an instance of the power of national myths[4] for all types of minds, and how they drive people to crazy behaviour, regardless of their relevance. In our case, a silly, extremely provincial (we should say parochial) Italian issue elicited an uncouth, delayed reaction. The imagined ancestry of modern Italy had been challenged, and the official hierarchies subverted. The perpetrators had to be scolded, and be sent away, if possible (Italian academy is being dismantled, jobs are few and far between and the lobbies of established academicians award jobs by co-optation to those in the approved groups according to a rota, as everybody knows and nobody says. Exceptions are rare). Never mind that no one else, apart from us three Italian speakers, understood what was going on. Never mind that we were all scholars from fully capitalist countries.

It was a perfect instance of the more general, typical answers nationalists of all countries (developed and undeveloped) give to external observers in order to persevere in their behaviour: they say to you 'you don't know', and when they find out you do know they resort to a disapproving 'you don't understand'. Or, as said in the course of the book, it could also be seen as another attack against the mythical figure of the communist anarchist, the person who does not believe and does not submit. Certainly, one might also hypothesise, for the sake of conversation, that the lady truly believed that Manzoni was a good writer. But that would be hard to believe even for economists, notoriously a category of people who read very little in their own subject, let alone others.

In any case, this episode is just a practical illustration at the micro level of the way the metaphysics of capitalism works[5] – that is, in a fascistic way. In fact, if things were not transformed all the time into high, or moral, or economic, or ancestral, or mass, or institutional items, not even the dialectical functioning of the metaphysics could keep the lid on the boiling saucepan of the human body, intellect and emotions. Plus, it is precisely the fact that most of them are simply and plainly wrong questions that allows for continuous discussions, and for labile, temporary solutions to come up, only to be discarded at the next round of dialectical interaction. Manzoni's literary worth, for instance, would be evident if people's taste and judgement were not so boringly homogenised and socialised.

In fact, the whole point of a vulgarly dialectical intellectual environment is precisely that of erasing the possibility of existence for a definite right and a definite wrong, in the vulgar, Hegelian way. To that purpose, even material reality itself is erased from the mind's reach (Micocci, 2016). The individual is dispossessed of his/her responsibility, and consigned to a socialised metaphysics. He/she can only choose, as in microeconomics. Let us say it straight: *Homo oeconomicus*, to the chagrin of most heterodox economists, does exist in practice, and mainstream economics, unfortunately, perfectly captures and renders his/her machine-like inanity. All the rest follows.

Notes

1 Not all Muslim countries are capitalist. Those Muslim organisations that claim to oppose Western culture and capitalism operate through terrorism and the state, two typically Western capitalist inventions.
2 Manzoni stated, without any objection (who would care?), that in his dreadful *I Promessi Sposi* he took as his linguistic base the dialect of Tuscany, i.e. of Florence. Dante Alighieri had done so at his own risk centuries before.
3 Another negative influence the imposition of this writer has is that of teaching young Italians that writing means talking a lot without saying anything.
4 Also in this case, as usual, the myth is false, simply invented.
5 Just as the fascism discussion of this work is a macro-level application of the same framework. The two things belong to the same general argument.

Bibliography

Abse, T. (1993), 'The Triumph of the Leopard', *New Left Review*, 199: 3–28.

Aglietta, M. (2016), 'America's Slow Down', *New Left Review*, 100: 119–29.

Alvesson, M. (2013), *The Triumph of Emptiness*, Oxford: Oxford University Press.

Alvesson, M. (2012), 'Do We Have Something to Say? From Re-search to Roi-search and Back Again', *Organisation*, 20(1): 79–90.

Alvesson, M. and Spicer, A. (2016), '(Un)conditional Surrender? Why Do Professionals Willingly Comply with Managerialism', *Journal of Organisational Change Management*, 29(1): 29–45.

Ascherson, N. (2016), 'Hopping in His Matchbox', *London Review of Books*, 2 June, 23–4.

Balakrishnan, G. (2011), 'Geopolitics of Separation', *New Left Review*, 68: 57–72.

Bandini, M. (1957), *Cento Anni di Storia Agraria Italiana*, Rome: Edizioni Cinque Lune.

Bel, G. (2011), 'The First Privatization: Selling SOES and Privatizing Public Monopolies in Fascist Italy', *Cambridge Journal of Economics*, 35(5): 937–56.

Bel, G. (2006), 'The Coining of "Privatization" and Germany's National Socialist Party', *Journal of Economic Perspectives*, 20(3): 187–94.

Benn Michaels, W. (2008), 'Against Diversity', *New Left Review*, 52: 33–6.

Berson, J. (2014), 'The Quinoa Hack: A Critique', *New Left Review*, 85: 117–32.

Black, W.K. (2014), 'Exonerating Corporate Executives', *Challenge*, 57(1), January/February: 60–6.

Bourdieu, P. (1998), 'La précarité est aujourd'hui partout', in *Contre-feux*, Paris: Raisons d'agir: 96–102.

Braverman, H. (1974), *Labor and Monopoly Capital: The Degradation of Work in the Twentieth Century*, New York: Monthly Review Press.

Bryan, L.L. and Joyce, C. (2005), 'Big Corporations Must Make Sweeping Organizational Changes to Get the Best from Their Professionals', *McKinsey Quarterly*, 3, 16 August.

Burnham, J. (1942), *The Managerial Revolution*, New York: John Day Co.

Callinicos, A.T. (2003), *An Anti-Capitalist Manifesto*, Cambridge: Polity Press.

Cambridge Journal of Economics (2009), Special Issue: The Global Financial Crisis, 33(4): 531–869.

Cassirer, E. (1962), *The Myth of the State*, New Haven, CT: Yale University Press.

Chomsky, N. (1967), 'On Resistance,' *The New York Review of Books*, 7 December.

Coleman, L. (2004), 'The Frequency and Cost of Corporate Crisis', *Journal of Contingencies and Crisis Management*, 12(1), March.

Colletti, L. (1975), 'Marxism and the Dialectics', *New Left Review*, 93: 3–30.

Colletti, L. (1974), 'A Political and Philosophical Interview', *New Left Review*, 86: 34–52.

Cunliffe, A.L. (2009), 'Management, Managerialism and Managers', in Cunliffe, A.L., *A Very Short, Fairly Interesting and Reasonably Cheap Book About Management*, London: Sage: 8–50.

Davies, N. (2016), 'The New Neoliberalism', *New Left Review*, 101: 121–34.

D'Eramo, M. (2013), 'The New Oligarchy', *New Left Review*, 82: 5–28.

Debord, G. (2004), *La Società dello Spettacolo*, Milan: Baldini Castoldi Dalai.

Deetz, S.A. (1992), *Democracy in an Age of Corporate Colonization: Developments in Communication and the Politics of Everyday Life*, New York: State University of New York Press.

Della Volpe, G. (1969), *Logic as a Positive Science*, London: NLB.

Derrida, J. (1978), *Writing and Difference*, Chicago: University of Chicago Press.

Di Mario, F. (2015), 'The Monti Cabinet Reform of the Welfare State: Metaphysics of Inequality', *International Journal of Applied Economics and Econometrics*, 23(3): 68–98.

Di Mario, F. and Micocci, A. (in preparation), 'Smith's Invisible Hand: Controversy is Needed', *The Journal of Philosophical Economics*.

Di Mario, F. and Micocci, A. (2015), 'Smith's Invisible Hand: Controversy is Needed', *The European Society for the History of Economic Thought Conference* (ESHET), Rome: Roma Tre University, 14–16 May.

Dore, R. (2009), *Finanza Pigliatutto*, Bologna: Il Mulino.

Drucker, P.F. (1973), *Management: Tasks, Responsibilities, Practices*, New York: Harper & Row.

Drucker, P.F. (1942), *The Future of Industrial Man: A Conservative Approach*, the new York: John Day Co.

Einzig, P. (1933), *The Economic Foundations of Fascism*, London: Macmillan.

El Mostrador (2016), 'La receta 'fascista' de Starace para hacer negocios hace olas entre los que se opusieron a reorganización de Enersis', Santiago, 20 May. Available online at: www.elmostrador.cl/mercados/2016/05/20/la-receta-fascista-de-starace-para-hacer-negocios-hace-olas-entre-los-que-se-opusieron-a-reorganizacion-de-enersis/

Everett, D.L. (2016), *Dark Matter of the Mind: The Culturally Articulated Unconscious*, Chicago: University of Chicago Press.

Fisher R., Ury, W.L. and Patton, B. (1987), *Getting to Yes: Negotiating Agreement Without Giving In*, New York: Penguin.

Fleming, P. (2015), *The Mythology of Work How Capitalism Persists despite Itself*, London: Pluto Press.

Forst, R. (2010), 'To Tolerate Means to Insult: Toleration, Recognition, and Emancipation', in Van den Brink, B. and Owen, D. (eds), *Recognition and Power: Axel Honneth and the Tradition of Critical Social Theory*, Cambridge: Cambridge University Press.

Friedman, M. (1962), *Capitalism and Freedom*, Chicago: University of Chicago Press.

Galbraith, J.K. (2009), *The Predator State*, New York: Free Press.

Galbraith, J.K. (1983), *The New Industrial State*, Harmondsworth: Penguin.

Galbraith, J.K. (1972), *La Società Opulenta*, Turin: Universale Scientifica Boringhieri.

Galli, C. (2001), *Manuale di Storia del Pensiero Politico*, Bologna: Il Mulino.

Gallino, L. (2011), *Finanzcapitalismo*, Turin: Einaudi.

Gentile, E. (2005), *Fascismo Storia e Interpretazione*, Rome-Bari: Laterza.

Gentile, E. (1996), *Le Origini dell'Ideologia Fascista (1918–1925)*, Bologna: Il Mulino.

Goldberg, D.T. (2009), 'The Threat of Race: Reflections on Racial Neoliberalism', *American Sociological Review*, 77(2), March 2012: 268–94.

Goldstein, A. (2012), 'Revenge of the Managers: Labor Cost-Cutting and the Paradoxical Resurgence of Managerialism in the Shareholder Value Era, 1984 to 2001', *American Sociological Review*, 77(2): 268–94.

Grey, C. (1999), '"We are all Managers Now"; "We Always Were": On the Development and Demise of Management', *Journal of Management Studies*, 36(5): 561–85.

Grossi, G. (2011), *L'opinione Pubblica*, Rome-Bari: Laterza.

Gutstein, D. (2009), *Not a Conspiracy Theory: How Business Propaganda Is Hijacking Democracy*, Toronto: Key Porter.

Harris, B. (2014), 'Corporisation, Managerialism and the Death of the University Ideal in Australia', *Journal of Politics and Law*, 7(2): 63–80.

Harvey, D. (2005), *Breve Storia del Neoliberismo*, Milan: Il Saggiatore.

Harvey, D. (1989), *The Condition of Postmodernity: An Inquiry into the Conditions of Cultural Change*, Oxford: Blackwell: 141–72.

Hayek, F. (2001), *The Road to Serfdom*, London: Routledge. First published 1944.

Hegel, G.W.F. (2008), *Fenomenologia dello Spirito*, Turin: Einaudi.

Hoopes, J. (2003), 'Managerialism: Its History and Dangers', *Historically Speaking: The Bulletin of the Historical Society*, The Historical Society, 5 (1). Available at: www.bu.edu/historic/hs/september03.html#hoopes. Retrieved 25 May 2016.

Hyman, R. (1987), 'Strategy or Structure? Capital, Labour and Control', *Work, Employment and Society*, 1(1): 25–55.

Joseph, J. (2010), 'The Dynamics of Strategic Militant Managerialism: Analysis of a "Strike"', *The Indian Journal of Industrial Relations*, 45(4), April: 671–93.

Karlsson, J. (2012), *Organizational Misbehaviour in the Workplace: Narratives of Dignity and Resistance*, Basingtoke: Palgrave.

Karnali, A. (2009), 'The Bottom of the Pyramid Strategy for Reducing Poverty: A Failed Promise', DESA *Working Paper* No. 80. ST/ESA/2009/DWP/80, August.

Klikauer, T. (2015), 'What is Managerialism?', *Critical Sociology*, 41(7–8): 1103–19.

Klikauer, T. (2013), *Managerialism: Critique of an Ideology*, Basingstoke: Palgrave.

Kolditz, T. (2009), 'Why the Military Produces Great Leaders', *Harvard Business Review*, 6 February.

Locke, R.R. (2011), 'Reform of Financial Education in US Business Schools: An Historical View', *Real-World Economics Review*, 58: 95–112.

Locke, R.R. and Spender, J.C. (2011), *Confronting Managerialism: How the Business Elite and Their Schools Threw our Lives out of Balance*, London: Zed.

Magretta, J. (2012), *What Management Is: How It Works and Why It's Everyone's Business*, New York: Free Press.

Marcuse, H. (1967), *L'Uomo a Una Dimensione*, Turin: Einaudi.

Manifesto di Verona (1943), '1° Assemblea nazionale del Partito Fascista Repubblicano.', 17 November, Verona.

Marx, K. (1992), *Early Writings*, London: Penguin.

Marx, K. (1977), *Capital*, Vols 1, 2, 3, Moscow: Progress.

Marx. K. and Engels, F. (1975), 'Manifesto del Partito Comunista', in Marx, K. and Engels, F., *Selected Works*, Moscow: Progress.

Merker, N. (2009), *Filosofie del Populismo*, Rome-Bari: Laterza.

Micocci, A. (2016), *A Historical Political Economy of Capitalism: After Metaphysics*, London: Routledge.

Micocci, A. (2012), *Moderation and Revolution*, Lanham, MD: Lexington.

Micocci, A. (2011a), 'Marx and the Crisis: A Necessary Theoretical Premise', *International Journal of Political Economy*, 40(3): 72–82.

Micocci, A. (2011b), 'The Preponderance of Finance and the Present Crisis', *Studies in Political Economy*, 87: 49–64.

Micocci, A. (2009/10), *The Metaphysics of Capitalism*, Lanham, MD: Lexington.

Micocci, A. (2008), 'The Transformation Problem?', *International Journal of Applied Economics and Econometrics*, 16(1): 32–49.

Micocci, A. (2002), *Anti-Hegelian Reading of Economic Theory*, Lampeter: Mellen Press.

Mirowski, P. (2013), *Never Let a Serious Crisis Go to Waste*, London: Verso.

Mirowski, P. and Plehwe, D. (eds) (2009), *The Road from Mount Pelerin: The Making of the Neoliberal Thought Collective*, Cambridge, MA: Harvard University Press.

Moretti, F. and Pestre, D. (2015), 'Bankspeak: The Language of the World Bank Reports', *New Left Review*, 92: 75–99.

Mussolini, B. (1935), *La Dottrina del Fascismo*, Milan: U. Hoepli.

Mussolini, B. (1934), *Scritti e Discorsi di Benito Mussolini. L'Inizio della Nuova Politica (28 Oct.1922–31 Dicembre 1923)*, Milan: Hoepli.

Onaran, O., Stockhammer, E. and Grafl, L. (2011), 'Financial Statistics, Income Distribution and Aggregate Demand in the USA', *Cambridge Journal of Economics*, 35(4): 637–61.

Palma, G. (2009), 'The Revenge of the Market on the Rentiers: Why Neo-liberal Reports of the End of History Turned out to Be Premature', *Cambridge Journal of Economics*, 33(4): 829–69.

Panic, M. (2007), 'Does Europe Need Neoliberal Reforms?', *Cambridge Journal of Economics*, 31(1): 145–69.

Panitch, L. and Konings, M. (2009), 'Myths of Neoliberal Deregulation', *New Left Review*, 57: 67–83.

Pellicani, L. (2012), 'Fascism, Capitalism, Modernity', *European Journal of Political Theory*, 11(4): 394–409.

Peters, M.A. (2001). *Poststructuralism, Marxism, and Neoliberalism: Between Theory and Politics*, Lanham, MD: Rowman & Littlefield.

Poole, S. (2006), *Unspeak*, London: Little Brown.

Posner, R.A. (2010), *La Crisi nella Democrazia Capitalista*, Milan: Bocconi Editore.

Potter, G. (2015), 'Police Violence, Capital, and Neoliberalism', *Dialogue and Initiative*, 1(4): 19–27.

Preston, D. (2001), 'Managerialism and the Post Enlightenment Crisis of the British University', *Educational Philosophy and Theory*, 33(3–4): 343–63.

Reich, W. (1970), *The Mass Psychology of Fascism*, New York: Farrar, Straus and Giroux.

Rosenberg, A. (1934/2012), 'Fascism as Mass Movement', *Historical Materialism*, 20(1): 144–89.

Rosenthal, J. (1998), *The Myth of Dialectics*, London: Macmillan.

Samuels, W., Johnson, M.F. and Perry, W.H. (2014), *Erasing the Invisible Hand*, Cambridge: Cambridge University Press.

Scarpari, G. (2004), 'Una Rivista Dimenticata: Il Diritto Razzista', *Il Ponte*, LX(1), 112–45.

Schipper, S. (2011), 'Not the Market Has Failed, but the State. The Hegemony of Urban Neoliberalism in the Case of Frankfurt am Main during the Crisis 2008–2010', Paper presented at the International RC21 conference.

Schmitt, C. (2014), 'Hegel and Marx', *Historical Materialism*, 22(3/4): 383–93.

Schumpeter, J.A. (2013), *Teoria dello Sviluppo Economico*, Parma: Rizzoli ETAS.

Schumpeter, J.A. (1993) 'Il Futuro dell'Impresa Privata di Fronte alle Tendenze Socialiste Moderne' (1945), in Schumpeter, J.A., *L'Imprenditore e la Storia dell'Impresa Scritti 1927–1943*, Turin: Bollati Boringhieri.

Schumpeter, J.A. (1987), *Capitalism, Socialism and Democracy*, London: Unin. First published 1942.

Schumpeter, J.A. (1951), *Imperialism and Social Classes*, New York: Augustus M.Kelley.

Scott. W.G. and Hart, D.K. (1991), 'The Exhaustion of Managerialism in the Twentieth Century', *Society*, 28: 39–48.

Senior, Nassau W. (1838), *Political Economy*, London and Glasgow: R. Griffin and Co.

Smith, A. (2009), *The Theory of Moral Sentiments*, London: Penguin Classics.

Smith, A. (1999), *The Wealth of Nations*, 2 vols, London: Penguin Classics.

Smithin, J. (2016), 'Some Puzzles about Money, Finance and the Monetary Incentive', *Cambridge Journal of Economics*, 40(5): 1259–74.

Springer, S. (2014), 'Postneoliberalism?', *Review of Radical Political Economics*, 27 February: 1–13.

Springer, S. (2012), 'Neoliberalism as Discourse: Between Foucauldian Political Economy and Marxian Poststructuralism', *Critical Discourse Studies*, 9: 133–47.

Springer, S. (2010), 'Neoliberalism and Geography: Expansions, Variegations, Formations', *Geography Compass*, 4: 1025–38.

Standing, G. (2011), *The Precariat: The New Dangerous Class*, London: Bloomsbury Academic.

Sternhell, Z. (1993), *Nascita dell'Ideologia Fascista*, Milan: Baldini e Castoldi.

Sweezy, P.M. (1962), 'L'Idea della Rivoluzione Manageriale', in Sweezy, P.M., *Il Presente come Storia*, Turin: Einaudi.

Sylos Labini, P. (2004), *Torniamo ai Classici*, Rome-Bari: Laterza.

Taptiklis, T. (2005), 'After Managerialism, Emergence', *Complexity and Organization*, 7: 2–14.

Tesche, B. (2011), 'The Fetish of Geopolitics: Reply to Balakrishnan', *New Left Review*, 69: 81–100.

Wacquant, L. (2012), 'The Punitive Regulation of Poverty in the Neoliberal Age', *Criminal Justice Matters*, 89(1).

Wacquant, L. (2009), *Punishing the Poor: The Neoliberal Government of Social Insecurity*, Durham, NC: Duke University Press.

Wrenn, M.V. (2015), 'Money and Neoliberalism', *Cambridge Journal of Economics*, 39(5): 1231–43.

Index